MEDIAEVAL SOURCES
IN TRANSLATION

4

THE STORY
OF ABELARD'S ADVERSITIES

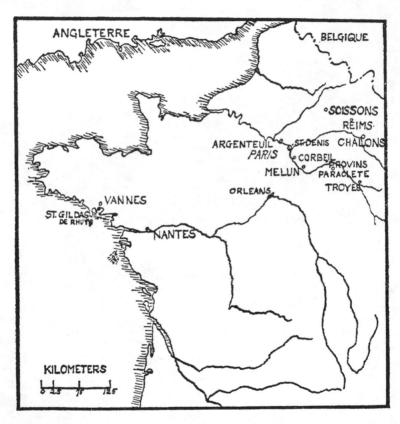

MAP OF WESTERN FRANCE
showing places mentioned in this work.

J. T. MUCKLE

THE STORY
OF ABELARD'S ADVERSITIES

A Translation with Notes of the
HISTORIA CALAMITATUM

with a preface by

ÉTIENNE GILSON

THE PONTIFICAL INSTITUTE OF MEDIAEVAL STUDIES

Library of Congress Cataloguing Data (Revised)

Abelard, Peter, 1079-1142.
  The story of Abelard's adversities; a translation with notes
of the Historia calamitatum [by] J. T. Muckle. With a pref. by
Etienne Gilson. [Rev. ed.] Toronto. Pontifical Institute of
Mediaeval Studies, 1964.

  (Mediaeval sources in translation ; 4 ISSN 0316-0874.)
  80 p.   map.   20 cm.
  ISBN 0-88844-253-X.

  I. Muckle, Joseph Thomas, 1887-1967, ed. and tr.
II. Pontifical Institute of Mediaeval Studies.   III. Title.
IV. Series.

PA8201.H4 1964   189'.4

First edition, 1954
Revised edition, 1964.

Pontifical Institute of Mediaeval Studies
59 Queen's Park Crescent East
Toronto, Ontario, Canada M5S 2C4

Printed in Canada.

CONTENTS

Abbreviations used in the Notes.

MGH = *Monumenta Germaniae Historica*
CSEL = *Corpus Scriptorum Ecclesiasticorum Latinorum*
PL = Migne, *Patrologia Latina*
PG = Migne, *Patrologia Graeca*

PREFACE

In the Latin literature of the Middle Ages, the story of Abelard's adversities occupies a place which can truly be called unique. In those days, men were not accustomed to write about themselves; even the memorable example of St. Augustine in his *Confessions* has found hardly any followers. Moreover, Augustine's masterpiece was a sort of spiritual autobiography rather than the story of his own life. Peter Abelard's intention was quite different. In the *Confessions,* the central figure of the story was God; Abelard occupies the very centre of his own narrative. As though trouble were his natural element and with his own career and his adventures as a knight-errant in the schools of philosophy, he was always willing to challenge any adversary. Add to this the extraordinary romance of his sentimental adventures, which he did not hesitate to relate with somewhat blunt honesty, and it will become quite apparent that, in the vast sea of philosophical and theological speculation which fills up the Latin Patrology of Migne, this tale of Abelard constitutes a most welcome island and port of call that no one would care to miss. Even apart from the unforgetable Heloise, many picturesque characters animate te scene about Abelard. The world of the twelfth-century schools, of whose daily life and routine we know so little, discloses some of its secrets and we find ourselves plunged in the midst of those concrete historical facts which Thomas Carlyle considered more precious than all historical generalities.

Such a text as this, therefore, should be read by all historians of the Middle Ages as a necessary source of information not only about one of the most outstanding figures of those times but also in those cases when the general interpretation of the period is at stake. The *Story of Abelard's Adversities* is as typical of the civilization of the Middle Ages as the *Autobiography* of Benvenuto Cellini is of the Renaissance. Philosophy and theology dominate the life of Abelard just as thoroughly as art dominates the life of the sixteenth-century Italian goldsmith; workshops are a natural setting for Cellini's life just as schools are the only fitting stage for the somewhat histrionic activities of Abelard. Yet, when all is said and done, the life and works of these two representative men differ much more than do their personalities. There is much more of human passion in the life of Abelard than one should expect to find there according to the accepted interpretation of the Middle Ages; on the other hand, there remains a great deal more of religion in the life of Benvenuto Cellini than should be there if that life were to fit the current view of the so-called paganism of the Renaissance. Were it to serve no other purpose than to occasion a new and more objective examination of these widely discussed notions, the publication of such a document as the present one should be welcomed gratefully—still more perhaps than most of its readers probably imagine. Only a scholar of many qualifications could undertake this sort of work and successfully bring it to completion.

Father J. T. Muckle, c.s.b., is just such a scholar. Countless adaptations and more or less counterfeit renderings of the correspondence of Abelard and Heloise have been published in modern times, particularly since the end of the seventeenth century. Many of them are quite entertaining pieces of literature; the only trouble is that they have so little to do with historical truth which, after all, is usually still more picturesque and unlikely than the wildest stretches of the imagination. To make this truth available to the English reading public, it was necessary, first of all, to proceed to a revision of the original text, something that had never been done since the time of Victor Cousin. For this was required a scholar equally at home in Classical and Mediaeval philology. Translating the Latin of Abelard was a still trickier task and only those who have not tried their hand at it will be deceived by its apparent simplicity. Last but not least, a great many problems of identification of persons and places had to be solved, some technical difficulties arising from philosophical terminology had to be cleared up. The foot-notes to the text of this translation, remarkable for their sobriety and precision, leave nothing to be desired in this respect.

This is no place to attempt an appreciation of the meaning and historical significance of this extraordinary document. Many good historians, all of them equally competent in their learning and sincere in their feelings, have set forth their personal views of the question without reaching too much agreement on most of the problems raised by the text. They do not agree on its authenticity, they question its historicity, some of them go so far as to doubt the very possibility of characters as strange as Abelard and Heloise. In fact, the nature of historical evidence is such that very few human documents are proof against all possible criticism. But is criticism itself always safer than the documents whose historicity it is so fond of questioning? Let us, therefore, enjoy reading such documents as this without spoiling our pleasure with pseudo-scientific scruples that are not likely to bring us nearer to historic reality. On the whole, it is a good thing that this world of ours, together with mankind and the course of its destiny, was created out of nothing by the Supreme Artist rather than imagined, according to the rules of verisimilitude, by the critical mind of some learned historian.

ÉTIENNE GILSON,
Pontifical Institute of Mediaeval Studies,
Toronto.

THE STORY OF ABELARD'S ADVERSITIES

(Abelard's Letter of Consolation to a Friend)

The experiences of others often serve to arouse or allay man's feelings better than words. And so to follow up the conversation in which I tried to console you at our meeting, I have decided to write you a letter of further encouragement based upon the experience of my own misfortunes so that when you compare your trials with mine you may consider them of little or no account and be stronger to endure them.

(The Place of his Birth)[1]

To begin, then, I was born in a town called Le Pallet[2] in Britanny near the border about eight miles I would say east of Nantes. I was lighthearted and had talent for letters, characteristics derived from my country and family. My father[3] was a man who had acquired some literary knowledge before he donned the uniform of a soldier and he retained such a liking for learning that he intended to procure for whatever sons he was to have a training in letters before their military service. And he carried out his purpose. As he loved me the more, being

---

[1] This and the other headings are put in parentheses as they were not written by Abelard since they are in the third person.

[2] Le Pallet is about twelve miles east and a little south of Nantes.

[3] Berengarius, as Abelard calls him later on. His mother's name was Lucia. There is documentary evidence that Abelard was the eldest of four boys; he mentions a sister also.

his first-born, so he saw to it that I was carefully instructed. The further I went in my studies and the more
easily I made progress, the more I became attached to
them and came to possess such a love of them that, giving
up in favor of my brothers the pomp of military glory
along with my right of inheritance and the other preroga-
tives of primogeniture, I renounced the field of Mars to
be brought up at the knee of Minerva. Since I preferred
the armor of logic to all the teaching of philosophy, I
exchanged all other arms for it and chose the contests of
disputation above the trophies of warfare. And so,
practising logic I wandered about the various provinces
wherever I heard the pursuit of this art was vigorous and
became thereby like the peripatetics.[4]

(Master William's Persecution of him)

I finally reached Paris where this branch of learning
was especially cultivated and enrolled under William of
Champeaux, a man who at that time was an outstanding
teacher in this branch both in reputation and in fact.
I remained under him some little time; at first I was
welcome but after a while he found me burdensome as
I began to question some of his statements and quite
often to argue against his position; sometimes I was
apparently the winner in the discussions. Those of my
fellow-students who were considered outstanding became

---

[4] John of Salisbury, *Metalog.* I, 5, refers to Abelard as *peripateticus palatinus.* Perhaps this passage first suggested the sobriquet *peripateticus;
palatinus* is likely a derivative of Palatium, his birthplace, no doubt with
the implications of its classical associations. In this one sentence Abelard
covers his early years away from home. This work was not meant to be
an autobiography.

the more deeply incensed at my conduct as they looked upon me as younger than they and as having spent less time at books. From this my troubles began and have plagued me to this day; and the more widespread my fame has become, the more has the jealousy of others been enkindled against me.

Finally it came about that with a presumption of ability beyond my years, I formed the ambition, young as I was, to be at the head of a school and to get as a location what was then the renowned town of Melun[5] which was also a royal seat. My above-mentioned master[6]

---

[5] The classical form is Melodunum (Caesar, *Bell. Gall.* VII, 58, 2), modern Melun. It was one of the several places of residence of Philip I. We do not know the exact year in which Abelard opened his school there. Some think it was in or about 1102. Cf. Remusat, *Abélard* I (Paris, 1855), p. 15; Tosti, *Storia di Abelardo* (Roma, 1887), p. 35. We know that Philip was in Paris in the summer of 1102 and in Bourges in October (cf. Maurice Prou, *Recueil des Actes de Philippe Ier, roi de France* (1059-1108) (Paris, 1908), pp. 355-358; 358-367). He probably passed through Melun to reach Bourges. Of course Abelard does not say that the king intervened against William. It was several years before 1108 when William established the Canons Regular in the Abbey of St. Victor and shortly entered himself. Cf. E. Michaud, *Guillaume de Champeaux et les écoles de Paris* (Paris, 1867), p. 245. Abelard left Melun, moved his school to Corbeil, and then spent several years at home building up his health. Upon his return to Paris, he found William had become a Canon Regular at St. Victor's. But we do not know how long he remained at Melun or at Corbeil or just how many years he was at home.

Abelard seems to be purposely vague in this and in the following sentence. It does not appear that he got permission from any ecclesiastical authority to open the school. How far was the *licentia docendi* required in the diocese of Paris at that time? Was there a *magister scholarum* in Paris that early? These are questions regarding which we have very few contemporary documents and the chief one is this treatise of Abelard. It seems that Abelard received the moral support of the temporal authorities and other men of influence and that he opened his school in the shadow of a royal castle to strengthen his position and to discourage any interference from church authorities.

[6] In the letters of Abelard and Heloise this term means the teacher of a school. In France, at any rate, down to Abelard's time, schools were either monastic or cathedral. The monk or cleric in charge of either

sensed this and in an attempt to have my school far removed from him he slyly used every means in his power before I withdrew from his school to hinder the furtherance of my plans and to deprive me of the place I had now arranged for. But some men of influence there were opposed to him and relying on their help I accomplished my purpose, as his open antipathy gained for me the support of many.

With the establishment of this my first school, my reputation in dialectical skill began to spread so that the fame not only of my former fellow-students but also of my master gradually lessened and went into eclipse. As a result, being more self-confident I transferred my school to Corbeil[7] nearer Paris that I might prove a greater embarrassment and offer more frequent challenges to debate.

But after the lapse of a comparatively short time, owing to the heavy strain of study, I fell sick and was forced to

---

class was called *magister*. But once Abelard started a school of his own. a third class emerged independent of a monastery or cathedral. Some decades later, the term has a stereotyped meaning; it denotes the diocesan officer who ruled over the schools of a city or diocese and who granted the *licentia docendi*. He was also called *scholasticus* and *cancellarius*. But the period from 1100-1150 was one of rapid development and transition. At the same time there are few contemporary documents pertaining to education. Care has to be exercised not to give this term the meaning in 1102 that it had later on. There is no mention of the authority of such an official when Abelard set up his schools in Melun, Corbeil and at St. Genevieve. William of Champeaux would, it seems to me, have appealed to him against Abelard if there had been any such official authority at that time. It should be remembered too that William was archdeacon of Paris, an officer with jurisdiction but whether over schools or not at that time is not known. He may well have been archdeacon when Abelard first studied under him.

[7] Corbeil, between Paris and Melun. Louis the Fat made it a royal fief just about this time and perhaps Abelard was again placing himself under the quasi-protection of the king. Cf. Remusat, *op. cit.*, p. 16, note.

return home; and though absent from France[8] for several years, all those who were anxious for instruction in logic kept eagerly trying to seek me out.

After a few years had passed I was well recovered from my illness. My teacher William, archdeacon[9] of Paris, had changed his state and entered the Order[10] of Regular Clerics for the purpose, it was said, of being considered more pious and thereby of gaining promotion to the

---

[8] Brittany did not become a part of the kingdom of France until late in the fifteenth century. It was ruled by a duke at this time.

[9] The archdeacon, originally a deacon and helper of the bishop of the diocese, came in the course of time to be a priest possessing extensive powers which he exercised, often independently of the bishop. From the tenth century until the decline began in the thirteenth century these powers were constantly increasing and varied from place to place so that it is impossible to define the archdeacon's rights just at this date (*ca.* 1110) since they were not based on written legal sources. Moreover it had now become customary to have several archdeacons in each diocese, each claiming jurisdiction over a fixed territory. Some light is thrown on the subject by a dispute which arose in 1126 between Stephen, bishop of Paris, and Theobald, his archdeacon. Appealed to by the archdeacon, Pope Honorius III appointed three cardinals to examine the affair. The decision which they rendered defining the archdeacon's rights is found in the *Recueil des historiens des Gaules et de la France* XV, p. 331. For a brief history of the archdeacon a useful reference is the article by A. Amanieu, 'archidiacre', *Dictionnaire de droit canonique* I, 948-1004. See also, A. H. Thompson, *Diocesan Organizatoin in the Middle Ages; Archdeacons and Rural Deans* (Oxford, 1944).

[10] During the eleventh and early twelfth century a spirit of reform and a fervent desire on the part of many of the secular clergy to lead a more apostolic and perfect life led to the foundation of communities of regular canons distinct on the one hand from the monks and on the other from the secular canons. Their manner of life comprising the practice of individual poverty was based in a general way on the *decreta Patrum* and was intended to be a return to what was considered the primitive clerical tradition in the Church. The teaching of St. Augustine especially as contained in the *regula beati Augustini* gradually came to play a role of increasing importance in the organization of this way of life so that many writers of the twelfth and thirteenth century identify the regular canons with the order of St. Augustine. Consult the excellent article with recent bibliography by Father Charles Derein, 'Vie commune, règle de saint Augustin et chanoines réguliers', *Revue d'histoire ecclésiastique* XLI, (1946), 365-406.

rank of a major prelacy, as happened when he was made bishop of Châlons.[11] But his taking the religious habit did not withdraw him from Paris or from his former philosophical pursuits. On the contrary, he immediately conducted a public school as formerly, right in the monastery to which he had gone for a life in religion.

At that time I returned to him to hear him lecturing on rhetoric. Among other essays at discussion I forced him by clear proofs from reasoning to change, yes, to abandon his old stand on universals. For he held the position on the common existence of universals that the same thing exists wholly and essentially in all individuals of a class and that there is no distinction of essence in them but only variety through multiplicity of accidents.[12]

---

[11] The life of William of Champeaux is not known in detail. He was born in the village of Champeaux near Melun about 1070 and died as bishop of Châlons-sur-Marne about 1120. He studied under Manegold of Lautenbach, Anselm of Laon and, strange to say, under the extreme nominalist Roscelin. He was teaching in the cathedral school of Paris when Abelard first studied under him. He became archdeacon of Paris and before 1108 retired to the religious centre of St. Victor which became an abbey of Canons Regular under him. Although he is rightly considered the founder of the school of St. Victor which afterwards became famous in the field of mystical theology under Hugh of St. Victor and his successors, William can be called the founder of the abbey only in a modified sense. There was already a community with a superior there. William became bishop in 1113.

[12] In philosophy William was a realist as this passage shows. He taught the 'community' (*communitas*) or common existence of universals, that is, that the essence of a class (species and genus) is a thing totally and simultaneously present in all its individual members; only the variety of accidents differentiates the individual members. According to Abelard, he changed his position by substituting 'indifferently' (*indifferenter*, without differentiation) for essentially (*essentialiter*). This term *indifferenter* has a technical meaning in mediaeval philosophy which was probably derived from its use in theological treatises on the Trinity. It is difficult to say just what it signifies here. Perhaps it means that the same thing (universal, species, genus) exists in all the individuals of its class but in a state of indetermination or without differentiation with respect to individuality. In the only text of William which we have, bearing on

He subsequently so modified his position as to assert that the same thing exists in individuals, not essentially, but without differentiation. This problem of universals has always been a moot point among dialectitians and of such magnitude that even Porphyry when writing about universals in his *Isagoge* did not venture to settle it but said[13] "it is a very deep question". Once William had corrected, yes under compulsion had abandoned his position, his lectures bogged down into such carelessness

the question, he says writing of the essence of God and the Trinity: "That we may exclude all ambiguity, you see that the two words *one* and *same* can be taken in two ways, according to indifference and according to identity of the same essence. According to indifference, as we say Peter and Paul are the same in this that they are men, for so far as pertains to their humanity (*humanitas,* manness), just as the former is rational, so also is the latter; and just as he is mortal, so also is the other. But if we would acknowledge the truth, there is not the same humanity in both since they are two men". *Guillemi Campellensis Sententiae vel Quaestiones XLVII* in G. Lefevre, *Les variations de Guillaume de Champeaux et la question des universaux* (Lille, 1898), p. 25. Does this passage constitute a third position of William? Some think so.

Abelard uses the term (*indifferenter*) again in his *Glosses on Porphyry;* writing of the realists he states: But since they would have all things so diverse from one another that none of them participates with another either in the same matter essentially or in the same form essentially, yet holding on to the universality of things they call things which are distinct (*discreta*) the same not essentially but indifferently (*indifferenter*), just as they say individual men who are distinct one from another are the same in manness (*homine*), that is, they do not differ in the nature of humanity (*humanitas,* manness) and the same men whom they call individuals according to their distinction, they call universals according to indifference and agreement of similitude. *Beiträge zur Geschichte der Philosophie des Mittelalters* (1918), Band 21, Heft 1, pp. 13-14. This passage is also found in R. McKeon, *Selections from Mediaeval Philosophers* I, (London, 1928), p. 228. Abelard also treats the question in his treatise *On genus and species,* in V. Cousin, *Ouvrages inédits d'Abélard,* pp. 515 ff.

13 Cf. Translation of Porphyry in Boethius, *In Porphyrium Commentariorum* I; PL 64, 82A. Porphyry, a Greek scholar and neoplatonist philosopher, was born at Tyre about 232 and died about 302. He studied at Rome under Plotinus and afterwards taught there for several years. Iamblichus was one of his pupils. Among his works are an *Introduction* (Latin *Isagoge*) *to the Categories* of Aristotle. It was translated by Victorinus and also by Boethius who wrote two commentaries on it.

that they could scarcely be called lectures on logic at all, as though the whole art were confined to the problem[14] of universals.

From then on my teaching gained such strength and prestige that those who formerly had somewhat vigorously championed the position of our master and had most forcefully attacked mine now flocked to my school and even he[15] who had taken over the chair of our master in the cathedral school of Paris offered his place to me that along with the other students he might follow my lectures right where our common master had held sway. Within a few days after my taking over the chair of dialectics, envy began to eat the heart out of my master and anguish to seize him to a degree I can hardly express. His seething soul did not long endure the misery which had taken hold of him before he cunningly attempted to depose me. And because there was nothing he could do against me personally, he set out by laying the basest charges to take the school away from him who had turned the chair over to me and to put another, one of my rivals, in that position. I then returned to Melun and once more set up my school there. And the more openly he attacked me

---

[14] The controversy over universals loomed large in mediaeval philosophy before the appearance of the New Logic and Latin translations of Avicenna and Averroes. In spite of his statement here, Abelard gave much attention to the problem: "Abailard's discussion of the universal naturally derives much from Boethius ... It is an interesting indication of the change of philosophic emphasis in six centuries that Boethius should have devoted two-thirds of his discussion to the utility of the study of logic while Abailard spends four-fifths of his commentary on that discussion on the intricacies of the problem of the universal", R. McKeon, *Selections from Medieval Philosophers* I (London, 1928), p. 204.

[15] Who he was is not known. Some think it was Robert of Melun but give no proof. See *Œuvres de Robert de Melun*, by R. M. Martin, o.p. (Louvain, 1932) I, VI, note 2.

in his jealousy, the more prestige he gave me, as the poet[16] says:

"What is highest is envy's mark; winds sweep the summits."

Not long afterwards, when he saw that nearly all men of sense had grave doubts about his piety and were loudly whispering about the sincerity of his conversion because he had not left the city, he transferred his community and school to a certain village outside the city. Immediately I returned to Paris from Melun hoping for peace henceforth so far as he was concerned. But because, as I have mentioned, he had put a rival in my former chair, I pitched camp for my school outside[17] the city on Mount St. Genevieve that I might, so to speak, lay siege to him who held my place. When my master heard of this, immediately and with no sense of propriety, he returned to the city and brought what students he had and his community back to his former monastery as if to raise the siege of his soldier whom he had abandoned. But while he meant to help him, he really greatly injured him. For, before, he had some students of a sort especially because of his lecturing on Priscian[18] on whom he was

---

16 Ovid, *De Remedio Amoris* I, 369.

17 Mont Ste. Geneviève became part of the city in 1211 under Philip Augustus.

18 There were two authors in early times named Priscian. 1. Priscian, the famous grammarian (*ca.* 500 A.D.) His most famous work is a treatise on grammar (*Institutiones grammaticae*) composed at Constantinople. It is primarily a treatise on Latin Grammar but shows its relation to Greek and quotes many examples from Greek. It was much used down through the Middle Ages until comparatively recent times. Published in Keil, *Grammatici Latini*, II and III. 2. Priscian the Lydian who composed for Justinian a solution of questions on psychology, physiology and the natural sciences. It was translated into Latin, likely by Scotus Erigena. This translation is found in *Supplementum Aristotelicum* I, 2, (Berlin 1886). Likely the first is meant here.

considered a great authority. But after his master moved in, he lost every last one of them and so had to give up his charge of the school. Not long afterwards, as if giving up hope of any worldly glory, he too entered a monastery.

The disputes which followed the return of my master to the city between my students and him and his students and the outcome which fortune gave to my students and to me among them, facts have long since told you. But to speak with due moderation, let me boldly repeat those words[19] of Ajax:

> "... If you ask the resuलt of this contest,
> I was not worsted by him."

and if I should keep silence, the fact would cry out and tell the outcome.

While all this was going on, my mother Lucia who was very dear to me made me return home. After the entrance of my father Berengarius into religious life, she made up her mind to do the same. After that was over, I returned to France especially to study divinity. My afore-mentioned master, William, now occupied the see of Châlons-sur-Marne. In this branch his master Anselm[20] of Laon at that time held preeminence because of his age.

---

[19] Ovid, *Metamorphoses* XIII, 89, 90.

[20] Anselm (Anselmus, more properly Ansellus) of Laon (died *ca.* 1117). Little or nothing is known with certitude of his education or the early part of his life. Likely he spent some time at Paris. Some have thought that he studied under St. Anselm at Bec. He taught theology at Laon with great distinction for many years. He became dean, chancellor and in his later years archdeacon of Laon. He and his brother Ralph conducted the school there. Some think Ralph taught the liberal arts. One should not form his estimate of Anselm from Abelard's bitter characterization. He was one of the greatest theologians of the time. Very many who became prominent in the field studied under him. The school of Laon, if not Anselm himself, played a prominent part in the

(Abelard goes to Master Anselm at Laon)

And so I enrolled under this old man whose great name rested on long practice rather than on ability or learning. If one in doubt about some point consulted him, he left him in greater doubt. He was a wonder in the minds of his listeners, but a nobody in the estimate of his questioners. He had a remarkable command of language, but it was despicable with respect to meaning and devoid of sense. While he kindled a fire, he filled his room with smoke but did not light it up. His tree appeared heavy with foliage to those viewing it from afar, but to those who came near and looked closely, it was found fruitless. And so when I went to this tree to gather fruit therefrom, I found that it was the fig tree which Our Lord cursed, or like the old oak to which Lucan[21] likened Pompey saying:

> "There he stood, the mere shadow
> of a great name, like an oak
> towering in a fruitful field."

Realizing this, I did not delay long in the idleness of his shadow. I went to his lecturse more and more irregu-

---

history of systematic theology. He is considered the compiler of part, at least, of the *glossa ordinaria* of the Bible. Bliemetzrieder, the editor, attributes to him the treatises *sententie divine pagine* (sentences from Holy Scripture) and *sententie Anselmi* published in *Beiträge zur Geschichte der Phil. des Mittelalters* (vol. 18, 1919) parts 2 and 3. Cf. L. F. Bliemetzrieder, 'L'œuvre de Anselme de Laon et la littérature théologique contemporaine' in *Recherches de Théologie ancienne et médiévale* (1933) 275 ff. A. Wilmart gives some data on his life in 'Un commentaire des Psaumes restitué à Anselme de Laon', *op. cit.*, 1936. See pp. 341-3. Cf. Beryl Smalley, *The Study of the Bible in the Middle Ages* (Oxford, 1941), pp. 33 ff. *Hist. litt. de la France* X, pp. 170-89.

21 *Pharsalia* I, 135-6.

larly, and for this the distinguished among his students were offended with me as despising a man of such renown; they secretly aroused him against me and by unfair suggestions brought him to become hostile towards me. One day after a session of *Sentences*,[22] we students started joking with one another. One of them, trying me, asked what I, who had studied only philosophical works, thought of the lectures on the sacred books. I replied that they were very beneficial since we thereby learn the way of salvation, but that I was greatly astonished that for those who were educated, to understand the commentaries of the saints, their writings or glosses were not enough without any other form of teaching. Many who were there derided me and asked if I could and would attempt to show them how. I replied that, if they wished, I was ready to try. Then they were loud in their cries of

---

[22] In the early Middle Ages, the study of and meditation on the Holy Scriptures (*lectio divina*) followed the traditional pattern of the monasteries from the time of St. Benedict. The text of a book of the bible or a choice selection of texts was followed verse by verse by an explanation and exposition (*glossa*) of some Father of the Church. Most of the moral and ascetical doctrine down to Abelard's time was derived in that way. But theology, as we understand it today, was beginning to take shape. A teacher (*magister*) taught by enunciating or citing truths or conclusions from Revelation (*sententiae*) and explained, developed, discussed and proved them from Scripture, tradition (especially as found in the Fathers); arguments from reason were also sometimes given; he also met objections and refuted erroneous doctrines. These 'sentences' were ordered in a plan *v.g.* the unity and trinity of God, His attributes, creation, angels, man, the fall, Incarnation, Redemption, etc., to constitute a systematic theology. Apparently Anselm was giving a course of this kind. It is exemplified in the *Sententiae divinae paginae* (Sentences from Holy Scripture) mentioned above (note 20). Abelard's position seems to imply that there is no need of such a method in the study of the Scriptures by a man of education. He can read and understand them with the help of a commentary (*expositor*) by himself. In view of Abelard's important place in the development of the scholastic method, it is difficult to see his consistency. Perhaps with his usual perspicacity, he is quite right when he says that most of his troubles were caused by his pride.

derision and exclaimed: "All right, take some commentary on some unusual passage of scripture, and let us put your claim to the test." All agreed on a very obscure passage of the prophet Ezechiel. Taking the commentary, I straightway invited them to come to hear me on the next day. They started to give me unsolicited advice saying that I should not hasten to such a task, but, inexperienced as I was, I should take a longer time to establish and confirm my interpretation. I indignantly replied that it was not my custom to advance through practice but through talent, adding that either they were not to object to coming to hear me at the time of my own choosing or else I would break the bargain.

At my first lecture there were only a few, as all considered it ridiculous that I, utterly unlearned in sacred science, should attempt this so hastily. But those who did attend thought my lecture so good that they praised it highly and constrained me to comment on the text in the same vein as that in which I had lectured. When those who had not attended heard this, they vied with one another in getting in on my second and third lectures, and all alike were anxious to make a copy of the glosses which I had begun on the first day.

(Anselm persecutes Abelard)

As a result, this old man, inspired by bitter envy and spurred on by the urgings of some against me, as I mentioned above, began to persecute me for my lectures in divinity with enmity no less than that of my master William for those in philosophy. There were then in the school of this aged man two students who appeared to excel, Alberic[23] of Rheims and Lotulph the Lombard, who were the more incensed against me as they thought highly of themselves. Moved especially by the suggestions of these two, as I afterwards learned, that old man arrogantly forbade me to continue in the place where he was teaching the work of interpretation which I had entered upon. He gave as an excuse that I might perhaps in that capacity write something erroneous, as I was unschooled in that branch, and the error would be imputed to him.[24] When the students heard this, they became highly indignant at this open manifestation of envy and spite such as no one had ever experienced before. And the more open it was, the more it redounded to my credit, and by his persecution, he made me more esteemed.

(Abelard at last enjoys Renown in Paris)

After a few days I returned to Paris and for some years enjoyed peaceful possession of the school of which, though

23 Alberic of Rheims and Lotulph were two of Abelard's chief opponents at the Council of Soissons as we shall see. Alberic became archdeacon of Rheims in 1113-14, and he and Lotulph conducted the school there. Alberic became Archbishop of Bourges in 1137. Cf. P. B. Gams, Series Episcoporum, p. 523. In 'Vita Hugonis abbatis Marchianensis' in Recueil des historiens des Gaules et de la France XIV, p. 398, we read of Alberic: As a lecturer he was thorough, charming and eloquent but not so in the solution of questions. Little is known of Lotulphus.

24 Here we find a magister forbidding Abelard to teach divinity and Abelard left Laon and went straight to Paris where he resumed the same course of lectures without molestation on that score. It will be recalled that William of Champeaux took no such action against Abelard a few years before. How explain this difference in his treatment at Paris? An easy explanation would be that Anselm was chancellor and perhaps archdeacon at the time. But surely there was a chancellor at Paris and William himself was archdeacon. And after a lapse of several years Abelard goes back and finds himself free to teach divinity there. All this only emphasizes the caution one should observe in making general statements about the organization and control of schools at that time.

long ago it had been yielded and turned over to me, I had
been deprived. As soon as I took over there, I was eager
to finish the commentary on Ezechiel begun at Laon.
My lectures proved so popular with my hearers that they
considered I had acquired no less charm in lecturing in
divinity than they had witnessed in philosophy. Through
desire for lectures in both branches, my students increased
greatly in number, and the financial gain and glory which
accrued to me you know well from report. But success
always puffs up fools and worldly repose weakens the
strength of one's mind and readily loosens its fiber
through carnal allurement. At a time when I considered
that I was the one philosopher in the world and had
nothing to fear from others, I, who up to that time had
lived most chastely, began to relax the reins on my
passions. And the more success I had in philosophy and
sacred science, the more I withdrew from philosophers
and divines through an unclean life. For it is well known
that philosophers, not to speak of divines—I mean men
attentive to the lessons of sacred scripture—were especially
adorned with the virtue of chastity. And while I was
laboring under my pride and lechery, God's grace provided a cure for each, though I willed it not, first for my
lechery by depriving me of the organs by which I practised it, then for my pride which my scholarship especially
nursed in me in accordance with the saying of St. Paul:
Knowledge puffs up. This was accomplished by humiliating
me through the burning of the book which was my
special glory.

I would have you know correctly the story of each cure,
just at it occurred, from the facts and not from hearsay.
I had always detested unclean harlots and my constant

attention to my books had kept me from frequent association with women of nobility and I knew little of society
among women in the world. But perverse fortune, as the
saying goes, by her blandishments found an easier way
to cast me down from the height of my glory, or rather
God in His goodness claimed me for Himself, a humbled
man instead of one most proud and forgetful of the grace
he had received.

*(How Abelard's Love for Heloise brought about a Fall
which afflicted both Body and Soul)*

There lived in Paris a maiden named Heloise, the
niece[25] of a canon named Fulbert, who from his deep love
for her was eager to have her advanced in all literary
pursuits possible. She was a lady of no mean appearance
while in literary excellence she was the first. And as gift
of letters is rare among women, so it had gained favor for
her and made her the most renowned woman in the whole
kingdom.

---

[25] Several theories have been brought forward regarding the parentage
of Heloise: one that she was of the noble house of Montmorency; another
that she was illegitimate. There is no documentary proof of either
assumption. Heloise herself in her letters to Abelard implies that her
family was of lowly estate. There is an entry in the necrology of the
Paraclete which gives her mother's name as Hersinde; under date of
December 1st we read: Hersinde the mother of our lady abbess; *Recueil
des historiens de la France. Obituaires de la province de Sens, IV, Diocèses de
Meaux et de Troyes*, p. 428. The name of her father is not known. There
is also an entry for December 26th on p. 429 of the same edition of the
necrology which reads: Hubert, a canon and uncle of lady Heloise.
Hubertus is probably a corruption of *Fulbertus*. The date of the birth of
Heloise is not known. Abelard tells us she was a girl (*adolescentula, puella*)
when he first met her. It is generally assumed that she was born about
1100 or 1101. She died in 1163 or 1164, likely on May 16. Cf. Enid
McLeod, *Heloise*, (London, 1938), notes 212, 220, pp. 287 ff.

I considered all the qualities which usually inspire lovers and decided she was just the one for me to join in love. I felt that this would be very easy to accomplish; I then enjoyed such renown and was so outstanding for my charm of youth that I feared no repulse by any woman whom I should deign to favor with my love. And I felt that this maiden would all the more readily yield to me as I knew she possessed and cherished a knowledge of letters; thereby we, though separated, could through interchange of missives live in each other's presence and, by writing more boldly than conversation permits, we could constantly engage in pleasant talks.

And so, all on fire with love for her, I sought opportunity to enable me to make her familiar with me by private and daily association, the more easily to win her over. To effect this, through the intervention of some friends, I arranged with her uncle to receive me at his own price into his home which was near my school on the pretext that the care of my household greatly interfered with my studies and proved too heavy a financial burden. He was a very avaricious man and also most anxious that his niece advance in her literary studies. Because of these two traits, I easily gained his assent and got what I desired since he was all eager for the money and considered that his niece would profit from my teaching. On this latter point he strongly urged me beyond my fondest hopes, acceding to my wishes and furthering my love. He put his niece entirely under my control that whenever I was free upon returning from school I might devote myself night and day to teaching her, telling me to use pressure if I found her remiss. I was astonished at his simplicity in this matter and would have been no more astounded if he had been giving over a tender lamb to a ravenous wolf. For when he handed her over to me not only to teach but to discipline, what else was he doing but giving free rein to my designs, and opportunity, even if I were not seeking it, easily to subdue her by threats and stripes if blandishments did not work? Two factors especially kept him from suspecting any wrongdoing, namely his fondness for his niece and my own reputation in the past for chastity.

What was the result? We were first together in one house and then one in mind. Under the pretext of work we made ourselves entirely free for love and the pursuit of her studies provided the secret privacy which love desired. We opened our books but more words of love than of the lesson asserted themselves. There was more kissing than teaching; my hands found themselves at her breasts more often than on the book. Love brought us to gaze into each other's eyes more than reading kept them on the text. And the better to prevent suspicion, 1 sometimes struck her not through anger or vexation but from love and affection which were beyond the sweetness of every ointment. No sign of love was omitted by us in our ardor and whatever unusual love could devise, that was added too. And the more such delights were new to us, the more ardently we indulged in them, and the less did we experience satiety. And the more these pleasures engaged me, the less time I had for philosophy and the less attention I gave to my school. It became wearisome for me to go there and equally hard to stay when I was using nightly vigils for love and the days for study. I became negligent and indifferent in my lectures so that nothing I said stemmed from my talent but I repeated everything from rote. I came simply to say again what had been said long ago and, if I composed any verses, the theme was of love and not of the secrets of philosophy. Many of these songs, as you yourself know, are still popular in various places and sung by people of like tastes. It is not easy even to realize the sadness, the expressed regrets and sorrow of my students when they saw the preoccupation and disturbance of my mind with such things.

Such a course could have escaped the notice of very few and of no one at all, I feel, except the man most disgraced by such base conduct, I mean the uncle of the maiden. When it was suggested to him at times by some, he could not believe it on account of his extreme love of his niece noted above and of my well-known chastity in the past. For it is hard for us to suspect those we love and the taint of suspicion of evil cannot exist along with strong affection. As St. Jerome says in his letter[26] to Sabinianus:

> "We are usually the last to know of the scandal in our own household and the sins of our wife and children remain hidden from us although they are the common gossip of the neighbors."

But at length we come to find out and recognize it and what is common knowledge cannot easily be kept from just one person.

And in the course of several months that is what happened with regard to us. Imagine his bitter sorrow when her uncle found it out. Imagine the grief of us lovers at being separated; how I was filled with shame and remorse over the maiden's trouble. Imagine the

[26] Epist. 147, 10; CSEL 56, I, 3, p. 327; PL 22, 1203.

sadness which flooded her soul from my sense of shame. Neither one of us complained of our own trials or bewailed our own misfortune but those of the other. The bodily separation became a strong link to bind our hearts together and our love became the more inflamed, denied opportunity. But shame gradually disappeared and made us more shameless and it became less as acts became easier. What the poet[27] tells us of Mars and Venus caught in the act happened also to us. For not long afterwards the girl noticed that she was pregnant and she wrote me about it with great exultation and asked what I thought should be done. One night, when her uncle was away, I secretly took her from his house, as we had arranged, and had her taken[28] directly to my native place. There she stayed with my sister until she gave birth to a boy whom she named Astralabe.

Upon his return, her uncle almost went mad and no one could appreciate except from experience the anguish which wrenched him or the shame he felt. He did not know what to do to me or by what plan he could waylay me. He was very much afraid that, if he maimed or killed me, his dear niece would pay for it in my native place. He could not get hold of me and coerce me any-

---

[27] Cf. Ovid, *Ars Amat.* II, 561 ff.; *Metamor.* IV, 169-189.

[28] In his second letter to Heloise (PL 178, 206A) Abelard tells us that she travelled to Britanny disguised as a nun. He gives no hint that he accompanied her.

Astralabe (Astrolabe) was not uncommon as a proper name in France in this period. Why it was given to this child I do not know. In an entry of the necrology of the Paraclete he is called Peter Astrolabe (in one *ms.* Astralabe). After Abelard's death, Heloise wrote to Peter the Venerable asking him to get a prebend for Astralabe from the bishop of Paris or elsewhere. Peter replied that he would try. There is some evidence that he became an abbot. Cf. McLeod, *op. cit.*, pp. 283-4.

where against my will especially since I was very much on my guard for I had no doubt that he would quickly attack me if he could or dared to. After a while I began to sympathize with him in his extreme anxiety and blamed myself for the deceit which love had wrought which was, as it were, a base betrayal. I went to see him and, begging forgiveness, promised to make whatever amends he decided on. I told him that whoever had felt the force of love or recalled to what a crash women from the beginning have brought even the greatest men would not be surprised at my fall. And further to appease him, I made an offer beyond his fondest hopes to make satisfaction by marrying her whom I had defiled, provided this be done secretly so that my reputation would not be damaged.[29] He agreed both by his own word and kiss of peace and by that of his backers. He thereby became on good terms with me which was what I asked but he did it only the more easily to betray me.

(The Arguments of Heloise against their proposed Marriage)

I straightway returned to my native land and brought back my beloved to marry her. She disapproved of the plan and tried to dissuade me from it on two counts, the risk involved and the disgrace I should incur. She stated with an oath that her uncle could never be placated by such satisfaction, as we afterwards found out. What

---

[29] Scholars have speculated on the reason that Abelard stipulated that the marriage be kept secret. See, amongst others, E. Gilson, *Héloïse et Abélard* (Paris, 1948), pp. 31 ff. Could not the chief reasons have been a marriage made 'necessary' because of the birth of Astralabe, and also that Abelard thereby put himself in the category of clerics who could not keep continent?

glory, she asked, would she derive from me since she would bring me to disgrace and humiliate both of us alike. What punishment would the world demand of her if· she deprived it of such a shining light? What curses, what loss to the Church, what weeping among philosophers would ensue from our marriage; how disgraceful, how lamentable would it be, if I, whom nature had produced for all, should devote myself to a woman and submit to such baseness! She utterly abhorred such a marriage which would prove a disgrace and a burden to me. She pointed out both the loss of my reputation and the hardships of marriage, which latter the Apostle exhorts us to avoid when he says:[30]

> "Art thou freed from a wife? Do not seek a wife. But if thou takest a wife, thou hast not sinned. And if a virgin marry, she has not sinned. Yet such will have tribulation of the flesh. But I spare you that ... I would have you free from care, etc."

But if I would not heed the advice of the Apostle and the exhortations of the saints on the great burden of marriage, she said, I should at least listen to the philosophers and pay attention to what has been written by them or of them on this matter. The saints in general have carefully done this to rebuke us. One instance is St. Jerome in his first book *Against Jovinianus*[31] when he recalls how Theophrastus carefully set forth in great detail the unbearable troubles and constant cares of marriage and confirmed by patent proofs his declaration that ·a philosopher should not marry and concludes his

---

30 *I Cor.* VII, 27, 28, 32.
31 Chapter 47; PL 23, 289A.

reasons based on the exhortation of philosophers by saying: "When Theophrastus so reasons... what Christian should not blush, etc.?" And again in the same work[32] St. Jerome goes on:

> "When Cicero, after divorcing Terentia, was requested by Hirtius to marry his sister, he emphatically declined saying that he could not devote himself to a wife and philosophy alike."

He did not say simply 'to devote himself' but added 'alike', not wishing to do anything which would compete with his zeal for philosophy.

To say no more about the hindrance to the study of philosophy,[33] she went on, consider the status of the dignified life. What could there be in common between scholars and wetnurses, writing desks and cradles, books, writing tablets and distaffs, styles, pens and spindles? Or who is there who is bent on sacred or philosophical reflection who could bear the wailing of babies, the silly lullabies of nurses to quiet them, the noisy horde of servants, both male and female; who could endure the constant degrading defilement of infants? You will say that the rich can do it whose palaces or mansions have private rooms, and who with their wealth do not feel expense and are not troubled with daily anxieties. But I answer that the status of philosophers is not that of millionaires and of those who, engrossed in riches and entangled in wordly cares, will have no time for sacred or philosophical studies.

---

32 *Ibid.* 291AB.
33 This and the following sentences smack of St. Jerome. Cf. *De perpetua Virginitate B. Mariae* 20; PL 23, 214AC. *Ep. 54 ad Furiam*, 4, 5; PL 22, 551-552; CSEL 51, I, 1, pp. 469-70. *Ep. 50 ad Dominionem;* PL 22, 516; CSEL *loc. cit.*, p. 394.

And so it is true to say that the great philosophers of old utterly despising the world fled rather than retired from it and renounced all pleasures that they might repose in the embrace of philosophy alone. The greatest of them, Seneca,[34] says in instructing Lucilius:

"You are not to pursue philosophy simply in your free time. Everything else is to be given up that we may devote ourselves to it for no length of time is long enough... It makes little difference whether you give up or interrupt the study of philosophy for, once it is interrupted, it does not abide... We must resist occupations which are not simply to be regulated but avoided."

What those among us who truly bear the name of monks endure for love of God, that they, the esteemed philosophers among the pagans, endured for love of philosophy. For among every people, whether Jew, Gentile or Christian, there have always been some who were outstanding for their faith and uprightness of life and who cut themselves off from the rank and file by their distinguished chastity and abstinence. Among the Jews of old there were the Nazarenes[35] who consecrated themselves to the Lord according to the Law. And there were also the sons of the Prophets, the followers[36] of Elias and Eliseus who, as St. Jerome[37] witnesses, are called monks in the Old Testament. Later on there were three classes of philosophers whom Josephus distinguishes in his *Antiquities*[38] calling some Pharisees, others Sadducees, still others

---

34 Epist. LXIII, 3.
35 Cf. *Numbers* VI, 21; *Judges* XVI, 17; *Amos* II, 11.
36 Cf. *IV Kings* VI, 1.
37 *Ep.* CXXV, 7; PL 22, 1076; CSEL 56, I, 3, p. 125. Cf. also *Ep.* LVIII, 5; PL 22, 583; CSEL 54, I, 1, p. 534.
38 XVIII, 1, 11.

Essenes. Among us there are the monks who imitate the
common life of the apostles or the earlier life of solitude
of John the Baptist.[39] And among the Gentiles, as we
have mentioned, there are the philosophers. For the
term wisdom or philosophy was used to refer not so much
to acquisition of knowledge as to a religious life as we
learn from the first use of it and from the testimony of
the saints themselves.

In line with this, St. Augustine in the eighth book[40]
of his *City of God* distinguishes the classes of philosophers:

> "The Italians had Pythagoras of Samos as the founder of
> their school who, it is said, first used the term philosophy. For
> before him, anyone who appeared to be outstanding by a
> praiseworthy manner of life was called a sage. But when he
> was asked what his profession was, he answered that he was a
> philosopher, that is to say, one who pursues and loves wisdom;
> it seemed to him that to say that such a one was already a wise
> man would be the height of arrogance."

And so in this passage where he says "appeared to be outstanding by a praiseworthy manner of life, etc.", he clearly
shows that the wise men, that is, the philosophers, among
the Gentiles were so called in praise of their life rather
than of their knowledge. How temperately and chastely
they lived is not for me to adduce from instances lest I
appear to teach Minerva[41] herself.

Now, she continued, if lay people and pagans so lived,
men who were bound by no religious profession, what
should you, a cleric[42] and canon, do to avoid preferring

---

39 Cf. *Mark* I, 2, ff.
40 VIII, 2; CSEL 40, p. 355.
41 The goddess of wisdom.
42 It is certain that Abelard was a priest when he was abbot of St.
Gildas, for he tells us toward the end of this letter that attempts were

base pleasure to sacred duties lest such a Charybdis drag you down headlong and you shamelessly and irrevocably swamp yourself in such obscenities. And if you do not regard the privilege of cleric, at least uphold the dignity of philosopher. If you despise reverence for God, let the love of uprightness at least restrain your shamelessness. Recall that Socrates had a wife, and the degrading incident by which he atoned for this defilement of philosophy to put others on their guard by his experience.

made on his life by putting poison in his chalice for Mass. It is not known when he was ordained a priest. Perhaps he began the study of theology with Holy Orders in view, especially if he intended to teach theology.

The words here, *clericus et canonicus*, indicate that he was not a priest at this time for the term cleric alone in the writings of the age usually means one who is only tonsured or at most has Minor Orders. If he had been in Major Orders, his rank would most likely have been added. In all probability, he was ordained priest some time after his marriage and after both he and Heloise had taken the vow of chastity in religion. A married man can by dispensation be ordained priest today provided his wife has taken a solemn vow of chastity in religion.

For reference to the legislation of the time relative to the marriage of clerics and canons, see the article by T. P. McLaughlin: 'The Prohibition of Marriage Against Canons in the Early Twelfth Century,' *Mediaeval Studies* III (1941), 94-100. A priest, deacon or subdeacon could validly contract marriage, but he forfeited his benefice thereby. A cleric in Minor Orders could marry and retain his benefice. A canon of any clerical rank lost his benefice if he married; that would explain the force of the clause: *ne divinis officiis turpis praeferas voluptates.*

When was Abelard made a canon and of what churches? We do not know. We know from a letter of Heloise, as will be seen, that he was head of the school in Paris at this time. Perhaps a canonry was attached to this office as Remusat thinks (*op. cit.*, I, p. 39). But there is no positive proof that he was a canon of Paris, although he likely was; on the other hand there is some evidence that he was canon of Sens, Tours and also of Chartres. Duchesne thinks he was canon of Sens and not of Paris. Father McLaughlin, *art. cit.*, 99, n. 40, is of the opinion that, apart from the Canons Regular who were bound by the law of celibacy the same as monks, there were two classes of secular canons: the first, those composing a Cathedral Chapter; second, those not belonging to a chapter.

Is it not possible that at that time a cleric could be a canon, without a benefice, of several churches, either at the same time or successively?

Jerome himself in his first book *Against Jovinianus*[43] brings this out when writing of Socrates:

> "Once, after he had withstood numberless words of invective which Xanthippe hurled against him from the upper story, she threw some filthy water down upon him; Socrates wiped his head and exclaimed: 'I knew that a shower would follow such rumblings'."

Heloise went on to point out what a risk it would be for me to take her back and that it would be dearer to her and more honorable to me to be called my lover than my wife so that her charm alone would keep me for her, not the force of a nuptial bond; she also stated that the joys of our meeting after separation would be the more delightful as they were rare. When she could not divert me from my mad scheme by such arguments of exhortation and discussion and could not bear to offend me, she sighed deeply and in tears ended her final appeal as follows: "If we do this, one fate finally awaits us: we shall both be ruined and sorrow will thereby pierce our hearts equal in intensity to the love with which they are now aflame." And, as all the world knows, she was possessed of the spirit of prophecy in this statement.

And so when the infant was born we entrusted it to my sister and returned secretly to Paris. After a few days, we spent a night in a secret vigil of prayer in a church and early on the following day we were joined by the nuptial blessing in the presence of her uncle and some of his and our friends. We straightway separated and left secretly. After that we saw each other only rarely and then on the quiet, hiding by dissimulation what we had done.

---

43 I, 48; PL 23, 291BC.

But her uncle and the members of his household seeking solace for his disgrace began to make our marriage public and thereby to break the word they had given regarding it. Heloise on her part cursed and swore that it was a lie. Her uncle became strongly aroused and kept heaping abuse upon her. When I found this out, I sent her to the convent of nuns in a town near Paris called Argenteuil where as a young girl she had been brought up and received instruction. I had a religious habit, all except the veil,[44] made for her and had her vested in it.

When her uncle and his kinsmen heard of this they considered that now I had fooled them and that by making her a nun I wanted easily to get rid of her. They became strongly incensed against me and formed a conspiracy. One night when I was sound asleep in an inner room of my lodgings, by bribing my attendant they wrought vengeance upon me in a cruel and shameful manner and one which the world with great astonishment abhorred, namely, they cut off the organs by which I had committed the deed which they deplored. They immediately fled but two of them were caught and had their eyes put out and were castrated; one of these was my servant already mentioned who while in my service was brought by greed to betray me.

When morning came, the whole city flocked to me and it is hard, yes impossible, to describe the astonishment which stunned them, the wailing they uttered, the shouting which irritated me and the moaning which upset me. The clerics and especially my students by

---

[44] She took the veil later when she formally became a nun of the convent; see *infra*.

their excessive lamentation and wailing pained me so that I endured more from their expressions of sympathy than from the suffering caused by the mutilation. I felt the embarrassment more than the wound and the shame was harder to bear than the pain. I fell to thinking how great had been my renown and in how easy and base a way this had been brought low and utterly destroyed; how by a just judgment of God I had been afflicted in that part of my body by which I had sinned; how just was the betrayal by which he whom I had first betrayed paid me back; how my rivals would extol such a fair retribution; how great would be the sorrow and lasting grief which my mutilation would cause my parents and friends; with what speed the news of this extraordinary mark of disgrace would spread throughout the world; what course could I follow; how could I face the public to be pointed at by all with a finger of scorn, to be insulted by every tongue and to become a monstrosity and a spectacle to all the world.

This also caused me no little confusion that according to the letter of the Law,[45] which kills, God so abominated eunuchs that men who had their testicles cut off or bruised were forbidden as offensive and unclean[46] to enter

---

[45] Notice that Abelard does not refer to any ecclesiastical law preventing eunuchs as such from being ordained or from exercising the duties of the ministry. It was men who had been guilty of self-mutilation only who incurred an irregularity *ex delicto* as they do today. Cf. *Codex Iuris Canonici* 986, 5.

For legislation on the matter previous to Abelard's time, cf. Ivo of Chartres, *Decretum*, Pars VI, Cap. 374; *Panormia* III, 56; PL 161, 523, 1143; Gratian, *Decretum*, Dist. IV, Canon 4: *Canones Apostolorum* XXI, XXII, XXIII in *Ecclesiae Occidentalis Monumenta Iuris Antiquissima* I (C. H. Turner, Oxford, 1899), p. 117; Council of Nice, Canon I; *ibid.* p. 112.

[46] No one who had any serious blemish could become a priest. Cf. *Lev.* XXI, 21.

a congregation and in sacrifice animals of like character were utterly rejected (*Lev.* chapter XXII):[47]

> "*You shall not offer to the Lord any beast that hath the testicles bruised or crushed or cut and taken away. (Deuteronomy,* chapter XXIII)[48]: *An eunuch, whose testicles are broken or cut away or yard cut off shall not enter into the Church of the Lord.*"

Filled as I was with such remorse, it was, I confess, confusion springing from shame rather than devotion the result of conversion, which drove me to the refuge of monastic cloister. Heloise meanwhile at my order had consented to take the veil and entered the convent. Both of us alike took the holy habit, I in the abbey[49] of St. Denis, she in the convent at Argenteuil mentioned above. I recall that many of her sympathizers tried to keep her, young as she was, from submitting to the yoke of monastic rule as an intolerable punishment. But it was in vain. Amid tears and sighs she broke forth as best she could into the famous complaint[50] of Cornelia:

> "O mighty husband, too good for such a wife, had Fortune such power over one so great? Why am I guilty of marrying you, if I was to bring you misery? Now accept the penalty— a penalty I willingly pay."

And while uttering these lines she hastened to the altar and straightway took from it the veil blessed by the bishop and bound herself in the presence of all to religious life.

Scarcely had I recovered from my mutilation, when

---

47 XXII, 24.
48 XXIII, 1.
49 The famous abbey of St. Denis in Paris.
50 Lucan, *Pharsalia* VIII, 94 ff.

clerics flocked to me, both those of my abbey and others from among my personal followers, and by constant entreaty kept insisting that what I had hitherto done through desire of money and praise I should now do through love of God, devote myself to study. They warned me that the talent the Lord had entrusted to me would be exacted with interest and urged me that, while I had before paid attention especially to the rich, I should henceforth be interested in instructing the poor; they argued that I should realize that the hand of the Lord had touched me especially that, being freed from the allurements of the flesh and the tumult of the world, I might devote myself to the study of letters and become a true philosopher not of the world but of God.

The life in the abbey which I entered was very worldly and disorderly and the abbot surpassed his monks by his base life and bad reputation as much as he did by dignity of office. I frequently and constantly kept speaking out both in public and private against their intolerable irregularities and thereby became offensive and unpopular above measure. They were very glad at the constant pressure of my followers and sought an opportunity of getting me out of the way.

After my supporters had long pressed it and caused embarrassment by their insistence, through the intervention of the abbot and my brother monks, I withdrew to a certain priory to give my time to conducting a school as I had done before. But such a crowd of pupils flocked there that the place became too small to house them and the land too little to sustain them.

While there I devoted myself especially to divinity in keeping with my state but did not give up entirely

instruction in the profane arts in which I had more
experience and which they especially asked of me. I used
it as a kind of hook by which I might draw them, enticed
by the flavor of philosophy, to the study of the true
philosophy, as it is recorded[51] by Eusebius of Origen, the
prince of Christian philosophers. But since the Lord had
apparently granted me as much favor in sacred scripture
as in profane, my school began to increase in both fields
and all the other schools to decline. As a result I aroused
the envy and hatred of the heads of the other schools
among whom there were two especially who spoke out
against me to my back in every way possible and kept
objecting that it was quite contrary to the profession of
a monk to be engaged in the pursuit of secular literature;[52] they maintained that I had presumed to take a
chair in Sacred Science without having studied under a
master.[53] Their object was that all teaching in a school

---

51 *Hist. Eccles.* VI, 8.

52 There is no mention made of the study of secular literature in the
Rule of St. Benedict. But of course once it became the custom to ordain
some of the monks, some study was necessary. Cassiodorus established
secular studies in his monastery at Vivarium and this fact had at least an
indirect effect on Benedictine practice, as it provided an example. But
I am of the opinion that the emergence of special monastic centres of
study was a natural growth arising from circumstances of time, place and
individual propensities rather than its having been the result of a
Benedictine tradition going back to Cassiodorus. Charlemagne's legislation prescribing establishment of cathedral and extension of monastic
schools doubtless gave the movement impetus. Could not the Irish
monasteries, especially Irish foundations on the continent, also have
influenced Benedictine practice in this matter? For the moot question
concerning intellectual pursuits and the Benedictine tradition throughout
the centuries, cf. Dom J. Mabillon, *Tractatus de Studiis Monasticis*, three
volumes (Venice, 1732); Dom Cuthbert Butler, *Benedictine Monachism*
(London, 1924), pp. 332 ff.; T. P. McLaughlin, *Le très ancien droit monas-
tique de l'occident* (Paris, 1935), pp. 111 ff.; Dom John Chapman, *Downside
Review* XXXVIII (1919), 84 ff.; Butler, *ibid.*, XLVIII (1930), 191 ff.

53 The phrase *sine magistro* likely means 'without having studied under

be forbidden to me and to effect this they constantly kept pressing bishops,[54] archbishops, abbots and all persons prominent in religion within reach.

As chance would have it I first gave myself to discuss the foundation of our faith by analogies from reason, and composed for my students a theological tractate,[55] *On the Unity and Trinity of God.* They had kept asking of me rational and philosophical expositions and insisting on what could be understood and not mere declarations, saying that a flow of words is useless if reason does not follow them, that nothing is believed unless it first be understood and that it is ridiculous for a man to proclaim to others what neither he nor his pupils can grasp by their intelligence. Such a man, they said, was branded[56] by the Lord as a blind leader of the blind. When most men saw and read this treatise, they were very pleased with it as it appeared to answer all questions alike on the subject. And since these questions seemed especially difficult, the subtlety of their solution appeared the greater.

Then my rivals, especially the two old plotters, Alberic and Lotulf, became greatly aroused and got a council to meet against me; since their masters and mine, William[57]

a teacher'. I do not think it warrants the conclusion drawn by some scholars that at that date one had to get permission from a *magister* to teach. If that had been the case, William of Champeaux would have used it when Abelard first broke with him and opened a school of his own at Melun, Corbeil and Mont Ste. Geneviève.

54 It would be quite natural for a twelfth century writer to put *episcopus* first. *Episcopus* is the generic term and we must remember that there had been a long contest to reduce the authority of metropolitans.

55 This work has been edited by H. Ostlender under the title 'Theologia Summi Boni' in *Beiträge zur Geschichte der Phil. des Mittelalters,* Band XXXV, Heft 2-3, 1939.

56 Cf. *Matt.* XV, 14.

57 It is generally accepted that William died in 1121 although Remusat, *op. cit.,* I, p. 84, n. 2, puts it '1119 ou 1121'. Gams, *Series Episcoporum,*

and Anselm, were dead, they sought to reign after them, and, as it were, to be their heirs. Since each of them was at the head of a school in Rheims, by their frequent suggestions, they persuaded their archbishop, Ralph, in association with Conan, bishop of Praeneste and legate in Gaul at the time, to open a meeting at Soissons which they called a Council; I was asked to come and bring with me the treatise on the Trinity which I had written. I agreed.

But before I arrived, the same two rivals had maligned me among the clergy and people with such success that on the day we came the people almost stoned me and a few of my disciples who accompanied me, saying that I had taught and written that there are three Gods, just as they had been brought to believe of me. As soon as I arrived, I went to the legate and gave him the treatise to examine and pass judgment on, offering to correct and to make amends for anything I had written or spoken at variance with Catholic Faith. He straightway told me to take it to the archbishop and those opponents of mine that they who had made the accusation might pass judgment on it. Thereby the saying: my[58] enemies are my judges was fulfilled in my case. Time and again they wen through and examined the treatise but, finding nothing which they dared to bring against me in the meeting, they put off to near the end of the council the condemnation of the book which they were eager for.

---

p. 534 puts his death in 1122, and P. Godet also puts it in the same year. Cf. Dict. de Théologie cath. VI, 2 (s.v.) col. 1977. But this is impossible since Abelard says he was already dead before the Council of Soissons in 1121.

58 Deut. XXXII, 31

Every day before the council opened, I expounded the Catholic Faith according to my writings to all in public and all who heard me commended with great appreciation both my expression and interpretation. When the people and clergy saw this, they began to say to one another: "*Behold*[59] *now he speaks openly* and no one utters a word against him. The council is rapidly drawing to a close which as we have heard was convoked especially against him. Do not the judges recognize that they and not he are wrong?" Thereby my opponents became day by day more incensed against me.

One day, with the intention of trapping me, Alberic accompanied by some of his students, came to me and after making some flattering preliminaries, said that he was puzzled at one thing he had noticed in my book, namely, that while God begat God, and there is only one God, yet I denied that God begat Himself. I immediately replied: "If you wish, I shall explain it." Alberic said in turn: "We are not interested in your rational explanation or interpretation but only in the words of your authorities." I answered: "Just turn the pages and you will find my authority." He had a copy of the book with him. I turned to a passage which I knew and which either he had not found or else he was looking only for what would tell against me. And God willed that I quickly found what I wanted. It was a sentence from the first book of St. Augustine, *De Trinitate*.[60] It reads:

> "He who thinks that God is of such power that He begot Himself errs the more as God does not so exist, nor does any spiritual or corporeal creature. For nothing whatever begets itself."

59 *John* VII, 26.
60 I, 1; PL 42, 820. This passage is in Ostlender's edition, *op. cit.*, p. 47.

When his disciples who were with him heard this they were dumbfounded and blushed with confusion. But he himself to cover up said: "Yes, but it is to be understood in the right way." I submitted that there was nothing new about his statement but it had no bearing on the present discussion for he asked for only the words, not the interpretation. I added that, if he was willing to listen to the interpretation and reason behind it, I was ready to show that according to its meaning he had fallen into the heresy of saying that He Who is the Father is the Son of Himself. When he heard this, like one in a rage, he resorted to threats and asserted that neither my logic nor my authorities would rescue me in this case. He then departed.

The last day of the council, before they resumed proceedings,[61] the legate and archbishop along with my rivals and some others had a long conference on what was to be decreed regarding me and my book which was the question especially for which they had been convoked. And since they had nothing before them either of my words or writings which they could charge against me, they kept silent for some little time or less openly attacked me. Then Geoffrey[62], bishop of Chartres, a man outstanding among the bishops both from his reputation for holiness and from the dignity of his see spoke as

[61] This indicates that other business had engaged the council. The *Acta* are not extant but in a *Life of St. Norbert* by a contemporary published by Roger Wilmans, MGH, *SS* XII, 663 ff., Chapter 11, there is mention of a council which Wilmans says is that of Soissons in 1121, and that it legislated against people attending Mass said by a married priest. This chapter is omitted in the later life.

[62] Cf. *Hist litt. de la France* XIII, pp. 82-87. Geoffrey was bishop of Chartres from 1116 to 1149. Cf. Gams, *op. cit.*, p. 536.

follows: "You know, my lords present here, that whatever the doctrine of this man be, it along with his talent has gained many supporters and followers among whomsoever he has studied and has greatly lessened the renown of his masters and ours so that, so to speak, his vine[63] extends its branches from sea to sea. If privately and without a trial you deal harshly with this man, which I do not think you will do, you should realize that, even though your decision be justifiable, you will offend many and that there will be numerous persons ready to come to his defense, especially since in the book before us we see nothing which should be publicly branded. And as Jerome[64] says: "courage when displayed always arouses jealousy and it is the mountain peaks[65] which the lightning strikes." Be careful not to add to his fame by doing violence to him and thereby bring on ourselves the charge of acting not through justice but envy, as the aforesaid doctor remarks:[66]

> "False rumor is soon repressed and the life which follows is the criterion of what has gone on before.

"But if you are disposed to act canonically against him, have his doctrine and writings brought before us and let him have an opportunity freely to answer when questioned so that, if convicted or if he confesses, he may be utterly silenced. At least such action would be in accordance with the statement of Nicodemus who, wanting to

---

[63] Cf. *Psalm* LXXIX, 12. This verse is applied to Abelard also in the letter sent to Innocent II by the Council of Sens in 1141 (or 1140). Cf. *Ottonis Fris., Gesta Frederici Imperatoris* I, 48; MGH, SS XX, 377.

[64] *Lib. Hebr. Quaest. in Genesim Praefatio;* PL 23, 983B.

[65] Cf. Horace, *Carmina*, II, 167.

[66] Epist. LIV, 13; PL 22, 556; CSEL 51, I, 1, p. 480.

free the Lord Himself, said:[67] *'Does our law judge a man unless it first give him a hearing and know what he does?'."*

When they heard Geoffrey, my opponents immediately cried out in a din: "Behold the advice of a wizard! He bids us to meet the verbosity of a man whose arguments and sophisms the whole world could not gainsay." But surely it was much more difficult to argue with Christ Whom Nicodemus urged them to hear according to the prescription of the Law.[67a]

When the bishop could not bring them to accept his proposal, he tried by another way to restrain their envy saying that those present were too few for the examination of a question of such importance and that the case demanded more exhaustive enquiry. His further suggestion in this matter, he went on, was simply that my abbot who was present take me back to my abbey, the monastery of St. Denis, and summon there some learned persons who after diligent enquiry would decide what was to be done. Both the legate and all the others assented to his last suggestion. Soon the legate arose to go to celebrate Mass before beginning the session. Through bishop Geoffrey he gave me the permission agreed upon of returning to my monastery, there to await the outcome of the arrangement.

Then my opponents, thinking they had accomplished nothing if the question was to be settled outside of his diocese where they could not use force, since they had

---

67 I know of no study of procedure in trials for heresy just at this time. For court procedure according to Gratian, cf. *Zeitschrift der Savigny-Stiftung für Rechtsgeschichte: kanonistische Abteilung* III, 239 ff. Cf. also Paul Hinschius, *System des katholischen Kirchenrechts mit besonderer Rücksicht auf Deutschland* V, (Berlin, 1869-97), pp. 431 ff., 449 ff.

67a *John* VII, 51.

little confidence in the justice of their cause, got the archbishop to see that it would be very discreditable to him if the case were transferred to another court and dangerous if I should be thereby acquitted. Straightway hurrying to the legate they got him to change his decision and induced him against his better judgment to condemn my book without any enquiry, to have it burned in the presence of all and to have me confined to perpetual enclosure in a different monastery. They said that it should be enough for the condemnation[68] of my treatise that I had presumed to read it in public and had myself given it to several to copy out although it had not been approved either by the Roman Pontiff or any other ecclesiastical authority. They added that it would redound greatly to the interests of the Christian faith if like presumption on the part of many others were forestalled by their treatment of me. Since the legate was less learned than his office required, he relied very much on the advice of the archbishop and he in turn on that of my opponents.

When the bishop of Chartres saw what was afoot, he straightway brought me news of their scheming and strongly exhorted me not to take it too hard as everybody could see that they were acting too harshly and that I could be sure that their violence proceeding from open envy would be very much to their discredit and to my advantage. He further advised me not to be at all disturbed by being confined within a monastic cloister

---

68 For censorship of books at this period with special reference to this passage, cf. G. B. Flahiff, C.S.B., 'Ecclesiastical Censorship of Books in the Twelfth Century', *Mediaeval Studies* IV (1942), 2 ff.

for he was sure that the legate himself who was ordering this under duress would set me scot-free after a few days when he got away from there. And so mingling his tears with mine, he, as best he could, consoled me.

(*The Burning of his Book*)

Accordingly, I was immediately summoned before the council, and with no preliminary discussion they compelled me with my own hand to cast my book into the fire, and it was burned up. But that some of my adversaries might appear to have something to say, one of them said in a low tone that he had found in my book the statement that the Father alone was omnipotent God. When the legate caught this remark, he was very surprised and said that he could not believe that even a stripling would make such an error since the common faith holds and professes that there are three omnipotents. When he heard this a certain head of a school, Thierry[69] by name, with a smile repeated the saying of Athanasius: "and[70] nevertheless there are not three omnipotents, but one omnipotent". His bishop[71] rebuked and tried to silence him as one guilty of *lèse-majesté*. But he boldly stood his ground and as though recalling the words of Daniel[72] answered: "*Are ye so foolish, ye children of Israel, that without examination or knowledge of the truth you have condemned a son[73] of Israel. Return to judgment,* on the

---

[69] Scholars generally agree that this is Thierry of Chartres, Cf. A. Clerval, *Les écoles de Chartres* (Chartres, 1895), p. 169.

[70] From the Athanasian Creed.

[71] Geoffrey of Leves. Cf. Clerval, *loc. cit.*

[72] Cf. *Daniel* XIII, 48-9.

[73] Daughter (Susanna) in the Vulgate.

judge himself pass judgment, you who have set up for
the establishment of the faith and the correction of error
a judge who, when he should judge, condemns himself
out of his own mouth; today God in His mercy openly
acquits an innocent man as He did Susanna of old from
her false accusers."

Then the archbishop arose and making the proper
changes confirmed the statement of the legate saying:
"Truly my lord, the Father is omnipotent, the Son is
omnipotent, the Holy Spirit is omnipotent, and he who
dissents from this and is openly at variance with it is not
to be listened to. And now, if it be your pleasure, it
would be well that this brother express his faith before
all that it may be properly approved or disapproved and
corrected". When I arose to profess and explain my faith
using my own words, my opponents declared that nothing
else was required than that I recite the Athanasian
Creed; a thing any boy could do. And that I might not
offer as an excuse that I did not know it, as if I were not
familiar with its wording from use, they had the text
brought to me to read. I read it as best I could amid
my sighs, sobs and tears. Then as one convicted of guilt,
I was handed over to the abbot[74] of St. Medard who was
present and dragged off to his cloister as to a prison. The
council immediately dissolved.

The abbot and monks of that monastery thought that

---

[74] Geoffrey. The prior was Goswin who attacked Abelard when he
was teaching at Mont Ste. Geneviève. Cf. *Ex Vita B. Gosvini; Recueil des
historiens des Gaules et de la France* XIV, p. 445. We also read there of this
monastery: The unlettered were sent there to be instructed, the licentious
to be corrected and the perverse to be subdued. For Geoffrey cf. *Hist.
litt. de la France* XII, c. 185 ff.

I would be there with them permanently and received me with expressions of great joy trying, but in vain, to console me by showing me every consideration. O God, who judges equity, with what bitterness of soul and anguish of mind I, in my madness, reproached You and in anger accused You often repeating the complaint of Blessed Anthony:[75] "Good Jesus, where were You?" I could then feel but cannot now express the grief which welled up within me, the shame that confounded me, the despair that upset me. I compared what I was then enduring with what I had formerly suffered in my body and counted myself the most wretched of men. I considered my former betrayal of little moment when compared to this injustice and I bemoaned the damage to my reputation far more than that to my body; the latter was the result of some sin while a sincere intention and love of our faith which compelled me to write had brought this open violence upon me.

When news of this cruel and harsh treatment spread around, all strongly censured it; each of those who had been present disclaimed any fault on his part and put the blame on the others so that even my rivals denied that the action taken had been upon their advice; the legate especially showed to everybody his detestation of the envy of the French in this matter. He straightway repented of his conduct and, after he had yielded to their envy under constraint for several days, had me brought back from the other monastery to my own where, as I mentioned above, everyone was hostile to me since their base life and shameless conduct made

---

[75] S. Athanasius, *Vita S. Antonii*, translated by Evagrius; PL 73, 132D.

them very suspicious of me and they found it hard to put up with me reproving them.

After a few months, fortune gave them an opportunity to set out to bring about my downfall. I happened one day to come across a statement of Bede in his *Commentary on the Acts of the Apostles* in which he said that Dionysius[76] the Areopagite was bishop of Corinth, not of Athens. This seemed in direct contradiction of their boastful claim that their Dionysius was the Areopagite who his history showed was bishop of Athens. When I saw this, I pointed out as in jest to some of the monks grouped about me this testimony of Bede which contradicted our tradition. They waxed very indignant and exclaimed that Bede was a mendacious writer and that their former abbot Hilduin[77] was a better authority; he had travelled in

---

[76] Both St. Jerome (*De Viris Ill.* 27; PL 23, 677B) and Eusebius (*Hist. Eccles.* IV, 21) speak of a Dionysius, bishop of Corinth. (By a blunder I wrote Athens instead of Corinth in my edition of the '*Historia*' p. 197, note 45.) Abelard wrote a letter to Abbot Adam in which he tries to solve the difficulty by suggesting that there were two bishops named Dionysius who were bishops of Corinth; that the Areopagite might have been one of these and that he had been bishop of Athens and Corinth at different times, and later was sent by St. Clement as apostle of the Gauls. Cf. *Abelard, Epistle* XI; PL 178, 344CD. H. Leclercq in his article on Paris in *Dictionnaire d'archéologie et liturgie* XIII, 1178 ff., gives the history of the popular legend. St. Denis the first bishop of Paris belongs to the third century; there is no proof that he was from the East. For a concise treatment of the question, cf. S. M. Crosby, *The Abbey of St. Denis* I (Yale U. Press, 1942), pp. 24 ff.

[77] Hilduinum, usually in texts Hildonium. Hildiun (d. 840) was abbot of St. Denis in Paris. He was commissioned by Louis the Pious in 834 to write a history of St. Denis; MGH, Epp. V, 327, 329. His *Vita sancti Dionysii* is printed in PL 106, 25 ff. In this work Hilduin was the first to state definitely in writing that Dionysius the Areopagite, converted by St. Paul, and St. Denis of Paris, were the same person. He also translated the works of Pseudo-Dionysius. His translation of the treatises *On the Divine Names* and *Mystical Theology*, and his Letters has been edited by G. Théry, o.p., *Études dionysiennes* I (Paris, 1937). For his

Greece for a long time investigating this question and, having arrived at the truth, had utterly removed all doubt when he wrote up the exploits of Dionysius.[78] When one of them threw at me the catch question as to what I thought of the discrepancy between Bede and Hilduin, I replied that I preferred the authority of Bede whose writing all the Latin churches held in esteem.

(*The Persecution of him by the Abbot[79] and his Brethren*)

The monks became very much aroused and began to exclaim that I showed openly that I had always hated their monastery and that I was now offering insult to the whole kingdom; by denying that the Areopagite was their patron, I would take away the honor which was their great glory. I replied that I did not deny their claim and that it made no difference to me whether he was the Areopagite or some one else, provided that he had won a bright crown with the Lord. Immediately they flocked to the Abbot and laid a charge against me. He was glad to hear it and rejoiced that he had some pretext for oppressing me for he was the more afraid of me as his life was worse than that of the rest. Then he called his council and the chapter of the brethren together and

translations, cf. Father Théry's articles, especially *Revue d'histoire de l'église de France* IX (1923), 23-40; in *Revue d'histoire ecclésiastique* XXI (1925), 33-50, 197-214; *Archives d'histoire doctrinale et littéraire du Moyen Age* (1936), 162 ff. Cf. also H. O. Taylor, *The Classical Heritage of the Middle Ages* (1929), pp. 82-90.

[78] Cf. *Sancti Dionysii Vita* MGH, Epp. Carol. V, 20, 10, p. 332; PL 106, 17D ff.

[79] Adam who was succeeded in 1122 by Suger. Cf. *Hist litt. de la France* XII, pp. 361 ff.; *Vita Sugerii Abbatis* by William, a disciple of Suger; PL 186, 1193 ff. As Abelard went there in 1121 and Adam died in 1122, this trouble must have happened to Abelard in that interval.

gravely threatened me saying that he would despatch me with haste to the king that he might wreak vengeance upon me as one who would take from him the glory and crown of his kingdom. The abbot ordered that meanwhile I was to be well guarded until he should hand me over to the king. In vain I offered to undergo the regular discipline for any fault I might have committed.

I became horrified at their villainy, and having suffered ill fortune so long I fell into deep despair, feeling that the whole world was conspiring against me. With the consent of certain brethren who pitied me and on the approbation of some of my disciples, I fled secretly at night and betook myself to the nearby territory of Count Theobald[80] where I had formerly stayed in a priory. I knew him fairly well and he sympathized with me in my hardships of which he had heard.

There I took up my abode in a priory of monks from Troyes in the town of Provins.[81] The prior, who was a friend of mine and loved me very much, welcomed me and looked after me with all diligence. My abbot happened to come one day to that town to transact some business with the count. When I heard of this, the prior and I went to the count and asked him to intercede with my abbot to get him to absolve me and give me permission to lead the monastic life wherever I found a suitable place. He and those with him deliberated on the matter

---

[80] The count in question was Theobald II, count at that time of Blois and Chartres. Provins is about 25 miles east of Melun.

[81] The priory of St. Ayoul at Provins which had been established in 1088 by monks from the monastery of St. Peter at Troyes. Cf. *Gallia Christiana* XII, c. 539; L. H. Cottineau, *Répertoire topo-bibliographique des abbayes et prieurés* II (Macon, 1937), col. 2368 *s.v.* Provins.

so as to give a reply to the count that very day before they departed. After deliberation they came to the conclusion that I meant to transfer to another abbey and that this would be an immeasurable dishonor to their own. For they looked upon it as a great distinction that I had entered their abbey for my religious life, as though I despised all the others; they claimed that a great humiliation would be theirs if I cast them aside and went over to others. As a result, they would not listen to me or the count. They went even further and threatened to excommunicate me unless I immediately returned. And they even forbade the prior with whom I had taken refuge to harbor me any longer under penalty[82] of sharing in my excommunication.

When we heard this, both the prior and I became greatly disturbed. The abbot departed holding fast to his obstinacy. In a few days he died.[83] Along with the bishop[84] of Meaux I went to his successor to get the permission I had sought from him. At first his successor would not yield but after I appealed to the king and his council through some friends, I finally got my request. Stephen,[85] who was then the steward of the king, called

---

[82] For penalties against those who received fugitive monks, cf. Gratian, *Decretum* D. 5, c. 5, *de poenit.;* D. 50, c. 69; C. 20, q. 3, c. 2, 3; C. 20, q. 4, c. 3; C. 18, q. 2, c. 16, 10; C. 11, q. 3, c. 3, 16, 17, 18, 28, 103, 110.

[83] Abbot Adam died in 1122 and was succeeded by Suger.

[84] Burchard was bishop of Meaux at that time, cf. P. B. Gams, *Series Episcoporum*, p. 575.

[85] Stephen de Garlande. He was a deacon. In *Mauriniacensis* (Morigny) *Monasterii Chronicon* II, PL 180, 152D, 153A; in L. Mirot's edition (Paris, 1907), pp. 42-3 we read of Stephen: He was chosen steward of the royal household. Back through generations it was unheard of that a deacon be in command of an army second only to the king. St. Bernard protested against his holding a secular position; cf. St. Bernard, *Epist.* LXXVIII, 11; PL 182, 197 A.

the abbot and his retinue aside and asked them why they wished to keep me with them against my will although it would serve no useful purpose since my life and theirs could never be compatible and scandal could so result. I knew it was the mind of the king's council that the more disorderly an abbey was, the more it relied on the king and became very useful for temporal gain, and so I believed that I could easily get the assent of the king and his council; and I got it. But that my monastery might not lose the renown it enjoyed through me, they granted me permission to go to any place of retirement I might choose, provided I did not make myself the subject of any abbey. Both parties agreed and confirmed the agreement in the presence of the king and his council.

And so I withdrew into a solitude in the district[86] of Troyes already known to me. There on a plot which was given to me I built with the approval of the bishop[87] of the diocese an oratory of reeds and thatch and called it the Holy Trinity. Secreted there with a certain cleric, I could sing the verse[88] to the Lord: *Lo, I have gone far off flying away; and I abode in the wilderness.*

When my former students discovered my whereabouts, they began to leave the cities and towns and to flock there to dwell with me in my solitude. Instead of large houses, they built cottages; instead of delicate foods, they lived on wild herbs and coarse bread; instead of soft beds, they used thatch and straw and for tables they heaped up sods so that you would think they were imitating the philos-

---

[86] In the parish of Quincey.
[87] Hatto. Cf. *Hist. litt. de la France* XII, 226 ff.
[88] *Psalm* LIV, 8.

ophers of old of whom Jerome in the second book of his
Against Jovinianus[89] writes:

"Through the five senses as through windows vice gains
entrance to the soul. The capital and citadel of the mind
cannot be taken unless the enemy break in through its gates...
If one finds delight in the sports of the circus, athletic contests,
the pantomime of actors, the beauty of women, the splendor
of jewels, clothes... and the like, the soul is taken captive
through the windows of the eyes and the words of the prophet
are fulfilled: *Death has come up through our windows*...

When through these portals the passions have wedged their
way into the citadel of our mind, what becomes of our liberty,
our fortitude, our thought of God? This is especially true
when the sense of touch rehearses past pleasures and by recalling sins forces the soul to take part in them and in a way to
repeat what it does not actually do... Influenced by such
considerations, many philosophers have abandoned the crowded
cities and the parks in the suburbs with their luxuriance, the
shade trees, the twitter of birds, the clear fountains, the mur-
muring brooks, and many other charms for the eye and ear,
lest through luxury and wealth the firmness of mind grow soft
and its purity be debauched. No good comes from frequently
gazing upon things which can one day lead to your enslave-
ment and in dallying with things which you would find it hard
to give up. For even the Pythagoreans shunned association of
this kind and used to dwell in the solitude of the deserts.
Moreover Plato himself, though a rich man—Diogenes[90] used
to track up his couch with muddy feet—in order to devote his
time to philosophy chose the Academy, a villa at a distance
from the city, which was a lonely and unhealthy spot. His
object was that through anxious care about their health, the
assaults of lust might be thwarted by his disciples and that they
might feel no pleasure except what came from their studies."

Such a life also the sons of the Prophets who followed
Eliseus are said to have lived. Jerome also speaks of them

---

[89] Chapter 8 ff.; PL 23, 310-2.
[90] Cf. Diogenes Laertius, *Vitae Philosophorum* VI, 26.

as the monks of that time when he writes[91] to Rusticus the monk:

> "The sons of the Prophets, the monks of the Old Testament, built huts for themselves by the waters of the Jordan; and forsaking the crowded cities lived on pulse and wild herbs."

Such were our disciples, who building their huts there by the river Arduzon appeared to be hermits rather than students.

The more scholars flocked to me and the harder the life they endured, under my teaching, the greater the glory which my rivals thought accrued to me and the greater the ignominy to them. And when they had done everything they could against me, they were grieved that all things worked together to my good, and as Jerome says:[92]

> "In hiding, as I was, far from the cities, the forum, the courts and crowds, as Quintilian[93] says, envy discovered me."

Secretly complaining and bemoaning among themselves they kept saying:[94] *"Behold the whole world has gone after him,* we have got nowhere persecuting him and gained for him greater renown. We have tried to blot out his name and we have made it better known. Behold, students, who have at hand in the cities everything they need, despise the comforts of city life and flock to a solitude with its poverty, and of their own accord become wretched."

---

91 *Ep.* CXXV, 7; CSEL 56, I, 3, p. 125; PL 22, 1076A.
92 *Liber Heb. Quaest. in Genesim;* PL 23, 984 A.
93 *Declamationes* XIII, 2.
94 *John* XII, 19.

At that time, unbearable poverty compelled me to run a school since[95] *to dig I was not able, and to beg I was ashamed.* And so having recourse to the profession I knew, I was driven to work with my voice instead of my hands. My students of their own accord provided everything necessary, both of food and clothing; they tilled the fields and defrayed the expenses of building so that no domestic care on my part interfered with my studies. And since our oratory could accommodate only part of them, they had to enlarge it by building an addition of stones and timbers. Although it had been first established and dedicated in the name of the Holy Trinity, I changed the name to that of the Paraclete because, having come as a refugee without hope, I had found there through God's grace some little consolation.

Upon hearing this, many were quite surprised, and some strongly blamed me saying that according to ancient custom it was not allowed to dedicate a church specially to the Holy Spirit any more than to the Father but to the Son alone or to the whole Trinity. They were led into making this charge against me especially because they erroneously thought there was no difference between the Paraclete and the Paraclete, the Spirit. But just as the Trinity and each person of the Trinity is called God and the helper, so too is the term Paraclete, that is comforter, correctly applied according to that saying[96] of the Apostle: *Blessed be God and Father of Our Lord Jesus Christ, the Father of mercies and the God of all comfort, Who comforts us in all our afflictions;* and as truth says: *and another Paraclete he will give unto you.*

95 *Luke* XVI, 3.
96 *II Cor.* I, 3, 4. *John* XIV, 16.

Moreover since every church is consecrated in the name of the Father, the Son and the Holy Spirit alike and there is no separate possession on the part of any one of them, what prevents that a house of God be named after the Father or the Holy Spirit just as after the Son? Who would make bold to erase from above the door the title of Him to whom the house belongs? And since the Son offered Himself as a sacrifice to the Father and the prayers in the celebration of Mass are specially directed to the Father, and the victim is immolated to Him, why does the altar not belong to Him to whom supplication and sacrifice are primarily made? Is it any more proper to say that the altar belongs to Him who is immolated than to Him to whom immolation is made? Who will admit that an altar is more properly called after the Cross or the Holy Sepulchre or St. Michael, John, Peter or some other saint who is neither immolated there nor is immolation made or prayers addressed to any of them? Even among the idolaters, altars and temples were said to belong only to those to whom they intended to address sacrifices and prayers. But perhaps some one will object that churches and altars are not to be dedicated to the Father because there is no external event which calls for special solemnity. But such reasoning takes away the privilege from the Trinity itself but not from the Holy Spirit since, from His advent,[97] He has His own

---

[97] Cf. St. Augustine, *Sermon* VIII, 13; PL 38, 73C: "The Lord rose, He ascended from hell but not yet into heaven: from that resurrection, from that ascension from hell fifty days elapse and then the Holy Spirit came, making as it were a birthday among us on that fiftieth day". Pentecost celebrates the event of the coming of the Holy Spirit which is, so to speak, His birthday on earth.

proper solemnity of Pentecost just as the Son from His
advent has the feast of His birth. For, as the Son was
sent into the world, so also was the Holy Spirit to the
disciples and therefore He has a claim to a proper
solemnity. In fact if we carefully consider apostolic
authority and the operation of the Spirit Himself, there
seems to be better reason to dedicate a temple to Him
than to one of the other Persons. For the Apostle ascribes
a spiritual temple not to either of the other two but only
to the Holy Spirit. He does not speak of a temple of the
Father or a temple of the Son as he does of the Holy
Spirit when he writes in the *First Epistle to the Corinth-
ians.*[98] *He who cleaves to the Lord is one spirit.* Likewise:
*Or do you not know that your members are the temple of the
Holy Spirit, who is in you, whom you have from God, and that
you are not your own?* Everyone knows that the sacraments
administered in the Church which confer divine gifts are
especially ascribed to the operation of divine grace which
means the Holy Spirit. In baptism, we are born again of
water and the Holy Spirit and then for the first time
become, as it were, the special temple of God! In its
consummation,[98a] moreover, the sevenfold grace of the
Spirit is given by which that temple of God is adorned
and dedicated. What wonder that we dedicate a material
temple to the Person to whom the Apostle specially
ascribes a spiritual one? To which Person is a church
more properly said to belong than to Him to whose

[98] *I Cor.* VI, 17, 19.
[98a] The Council of Elvira (*ca.* 300) calls the sacrament of confirmation
the perfecting of that of baptism. Cf. Canons 38.77, Hefele, *Histoire des
Conciles* I, pp. 242, 262. Cf. also the pseudo-Ambrosian *De Sacramentis*
(fourth century?) III, 2, 8; PL 16, 453 B.

operation all the benefits administered in the Church are specially ascribed? Moreover, we do not imply that when we first called our Oratory the Paraclete that we meant to dedicate it to one Person alone but simply, for the reason we gave above, to commemorate our consolation; and yet if we had done it in the sense generally supposed, it would have accorded with reason, if not with custom.

(The Persecution against Abelard on the part of certain Individuals who would be new Apostles)

I was dwelling in this place in bodily retirement though my fame was spreading throughout the whole world, like echo of poetic fable[99] which sends back its image, having sound but not substance. Since my former adversaries could avail nothing by themselves, they stirred up against me certain individuals, new Apostles,[100] in whom the world had great confidence. One of these claimed it as his glory that he had revived the life of Regular Canons, the other of monks. These men went up and down the countryside and in their preaching shamelessly kept backbiting me as best they could. For a time they made me an object of contempt with certain ecclesiastical and secular powers, questioning my orthodoxy and upright-ness of life so that they turned even my chief friends

---

[99] Cf. Ovid, *Metamor.* III, 359.

[100] The doctors of Paris who censured Abelard's works (PL 178, 109A) interpreted this passage as referring to St. Norbert and St. Bernard. But so far as our records go, it is difficult to find documentary evidence for this interpretation.

We have no sermons of St. Norbert or other texts which contain an attack on Abelard, and the passages from St. Bernard's works which criticize Abelard are written after 1135, the *terminus a quo* of this text. For a discussion of this question, see Appendix to my edition of 'Historia Calamitatum', *Mediaeval Studies* XII (1950), pp. 212-3.

from me; and if some kept any of their old esteem for
me, they pretended not to, through fear of those two.
God is my witness that whenever I learned of a meeting
of ecclesiastics, I supposed it was to condemn me. Like
one who expected to be struck by lightning, I was
straightway overcome with fear that like a heretic or one
irreligious I would be dragged before a council or syna-
gogue. And to compare a flea to a lion and an ant to an
elephant, my rivals persecuted me with no less venom
than did the heretics hound Athanasius of old. God
knows, I fell into such despair that I was ready to depart
from the Christian world and to go to the Saracens,
there, by paying whatever tribute was demanded, to live
a Christian life among the enemies of Christ. I thought
that they would be the better disposed towards me as they
would suspect from the charges made against me that I
was not a Christian and so would believe that I would
therefore be more easily induced to join their religion.

(*Abelard is elected an Abbot and the Reason why he accepted the Office*)

While I was being ceaselessly oppressed such dis-
turbing activities and while my last recourse was to flee
to Christ among His enemies, an opportunity presented
itself of getting away somewhat, as I thought, from these
plots. But as it turned out I fell in with Christians and
monks by far more savage and worse than Saracens. The
abbot of a certain monastery, St. Gildas de Rhuys[1] in the
diocese[2] of Vannes in Britanny died and by a unanimous

---

1 Cf. *Gallia christ.* XIV, 958 ff.
2 Morvanus was bishop of Vannes in 1125. Cf. Gams, *op. cit.*, p. 649.

choice of the brethren with the approval of the temporal ruler[3] I was elected. They readily got the endorsement of my abbot and fellow monks. And so the envy of the French drove me to the West just as that of the Romans did Jerome to the East.[4] God knows, I never would have given my consent, had it not been, as I have said, that I might in some way or other escape from the acts of oppression which without end I was enduring.

It is a barbarous country; I did not know the language;[5] the base and incorrigible life of the monks there was almost a legend among all, and the people of that country were rude and uncultured. And so just as a man, terrified by a sword hanging above him, hurls himself over a precipice and thereby in an instant escapes one form of death only to incur another, so I knowingly got away from one danger by running into another. There within hearing of the frightening sound of the roar of the sea where the last point of land afforded me no further refuge, I often in my prayers thought over the saying:[6] *To Thee have I cried from the ends of the earth when my heart was in anguish.* With what trepidation that undisciplined community whose direction I had undertaken tortured my heart night and day as I weighed the

---

[3] Conon IV was then duke of Brittany although this may well refer to a feudal lord, who by donation of land or otherwise had some voice in the appointment of the abbot. Abelard says the monks chose him with the consent of the temporal authority. Abelard became abbot of St. Gildas about 1125. Cf. D. Morice, *Histor. britan.* II, 92, for the catalogue of the abbots of St. Gildas.

[4] This probably refers to Jerome's departure for the East after the death of Pope Damasus.

[5] Abelard was a Breton but there were several dialects in Brittany. Le Pallet, his birth-place, was near the boundary line: the population likely was mixed; then, too, Abelard left there at an early age.

[6] *Psalm* LX, 3.

dangers both to body and soul, everyone, I think, now realizes. I felt certain that if I tried to force them to the life of rule to which they had been professed, it would be at the cost of my life; and yet if I did not do it to the best of my power, I would be damned. The abbye itself a certain tyrant, the most powerful in that district, had for a long time kept in subjugation to himself. He took advantage of the disorders there to convert to his own use the adjacent lands and to levy greater imposts on the monks than he would have on Jews subject to tribute.[7]

The monks kept pressing me for their daily needs although the community had nothing to give them; they had been supporting their concubines with their sons and daughters from their own purse. They were glad to see me upset by their demands and they kept stealing and taking away what they could get their hands on, so that, owing to my inability to minister to their needs, I would be compelled to cease insisting on discipline or get out. And since the barbarous population of that district was also undisciplined and lawless, I had no one to whom to

---

[7] In several countries, especially from late twelfth century on, Jews had to pay special imposts levied from time to time. Various causes contributed to the enactment of such measures: the spirit of the crusades reacted indirectly against the Jews; kings and princes used this means to raise money; the Jews practised usury, sometimes at exorbitant rates; in some instances they held extensive ownership of property, especially in cities. In France, Philip Augustus (1180-1223) confiscated their property and banished them from the royal domain for some years; they returned in 1198. I do not find any record of special imposts levied from the Jews in Northern France just at the time Abelard is writing; he is likely using the phrase in a general way and has not any particular local enactments in mind. Some information can be gained from Georg Caro, *Sozial und Wirtschafsgeschichte der Juden im Mittellalter und der Neuzeit* I (1924), pp. 351 ff.; S. W. Baron, *The Jewish Community* II (1942), pp. 246 ff.; J. H. Bridges, Oxford Essays (1857), *Jews of the Empire in the Middle Ages*, pp. 213 ff. (a biased work).

go for help as I was opposed to the behavior of all alike. The despot and his satellites constantly oppressed me from without and my brethren within kept plotting against me without ceasing so that the state of affairs proved that the saying[8] of the Apostle especially applied to me: *Conflicts without, anxieties within.*

I kept thinking over and bewailing the useless and wretched life I was leading; how fruitless it was to me and everybody else; I had formerly been of great service to clerics, but now, having deserted them for the sake of monks, I availed nothing either among them or the monks. I realized how all my beginnings, how all my undertakings and endeavors had come to naught and that against me of all men the reproach[9] could justly be made: *This man began to build and was not able to finish.* I was cast into deep despair when I recalled what I had fled from and realized what I had run into; considering my former troubles as of naught, I often said to myself amid sighs: justly do I suffer this since I deserted the Paraclete, that is the consoler, and thereby thrust myself into sure desolation, and to avoid threats ran into certain perils.

This further thought tortured me most that, having abandoned my Oratory, I was unable to provide, as I should, for the celebration of the Divine Office there since the extreme poverty of the place would scarcely support even one man. But the true Paraclete again brought me true comfort in my discouragement and made provision for the Oratory as might be expected for it was His own. It happened that my abbot of St. Denis had

8 *II Cor.* VII, 5.
9 *Luke* XIV, 30.

managed to acquire the abbey[10] at Argenteuil which I
have mentioned before and where Heloise now my sister
in Christ rather than wife had received the religious habit.
He accomplished this on the ground that of old it had
belonged to his monastery. He proceeded to expel the
community of nuns there of which my partner was
prioress. When they were being scattered as exiles to
various places, I saw that the Lord had given me opportunity of providing for my Oratory. Accordingly, I went
back there and invited Heloise and those of the nuns of
the same community who were loyal to her to come to the
Oratory. Upon their arrival I granted to them as a gift
the Oratory and all property connected with it. This
donation Pope Innocent II,[11] with the approval and
through the intercession of the local bishop,[12] by a document (*privilegium*) confirmed to them and their successors
in perpetuity.

At first they endured a life of privation and for a time
they were very discouraged. But God, whom they were
faithfully serving, in His mercy soon brought them
comfort. He proved Himself their true comforter by
making the people round about pity and be helpful to

10 The original foundation of Argenteuil went back to the time of
Clothair III. Whether it was from the first a convent for nuns or monks
is not known. Suger claimed he had read a charter which showed it
belonged to the Abbey of St. Denis from the time of Pepin. He
presented the claim to Rome and probably laid a charge of irregularity
of life against the nuns. By action of Pope Honorius II and King
Louis VI, the convent was transferred to the ownership of St. Denis in
1129. For a full account, see Enid McLeod, *Heloise* (London, 1938),
pp. 93-104.

11 About Nov. 28, 1131. Cf. PL 179, 114; Jaffé-Lowenfeld, *Regesta,*
7513; C. Charrier, *Héloïse dans l'histoire et dans la légende* (Paris, 1933),
pp. 261 ff. for this and confirmations by later popes of grants of property
to The Paraclete.

12 Hatto, bishop of Troyes. Cf. *Hist. litt. de la France* XII, p. 226.

them. And I think their worldly goods were multiplied, God knows, more within one year than they would have been in a hundred if I had stayed on.

For as woman is the weaker sex, so her dire need more readily arouses human sympathy and her life of virtue is the more pleasing to God and man. God granted such favor in the eyes of all to my sister who was over the other nuns that bishops loved her as a daughter, abbots[13] as a sister, the laity as their mother and all alike admired her spirit of religion, her prudence and her great meekness in every circumstance, a virtue inseparable from patience. And the more rarely she presented herself to the public, that she might without distraction within her cloister give herself to prayer and meditation on holy things, the more eagerly the world outside demanded her presence and the advice of her spiritual conversation.

(The Accusation of Lewdness against Abelard)

While all their neighbors began to find fault with me on the ground that I did not go to succor these nuns in their need according to my power and obligation, saying that I could easily do so at least by my preaching, I began to visit them quite often to help them in any way I could. As a result, gossip engendered by envy arose, and what sincere charity impelled me to do, that my calumniators with their usual perverseness shamelessly condemned, hurling the charge that I was still in the power of a lingering delight in carnal lust and could

---

[13] St. Bernard visited her monastery later on and wrote her a letter. Peter the Venerable wrote her after the death of Abelard. Cf. McLeod, op. cit., pp. 127, 202; Charrier, op. cit., p. 281 ff.

scarcely or never endure the absence of my old lover.
I frequently thought of the complaint[14] of St. Jerome
when he writes to Asella about false friends:

> "My only crime is my sex and even on that score I am not
> charged except when Paula goes to Jerusalem... and again:
> Before I came to know the family of saintly Paula, all Rome
> resounded with expressions of good-will towards me. Nearly
> everyone deemed me worthy of becoming pope... But I know
> how by good and evil report to arrive at the kingdom of
> heaven."

When, I say, I brought to mind the malicious detraction levelled against so great a man, I derived therefrom
no little consolation as I thought to myself: if my
enemies found in me so great a cause for suspicion, what
detraction would they heap upon me! But now that God
in His mercy has freed me from any cause for such
suspicion by taking away from me the power to commit
base acts, how is it that suspicion remains? What is the
meaning of this latest shameless charge? For my condition
removes in the minds of all every suspicion of base
conduct. So true is this that whoever desired to keep
careful guard over their women put them under the
protection of eunuchs, as sacred history tells of Esther[15]
and the other consorts of King Assuerus. We read[16] also
that it was a eunuch of Queen Candace, a man of
authority and in charge of all her treasures, whom the
angel sent the Apostle Philip to convert and baptize.
It has always been true of modest and upright women,
that the further they kept themselves from any suspicion

---

14 Epist. XLV, 2; CSEL 54, I, 1, p. 324; PL 22, 481, 484.
15 Cf. *Esther* II, 3.
16 *Acts* VIII, 27 ff.

on this score, the greater were the dignity and esteem they enjoyed. And it was to forestall any such suspicion that, as it is related in the sixth book of *Ecclesiastical History*,[17] Origen the greatest Christian philosopher laid hands on himself when he undertook the instruction of women in holy doctrine. I considered that on this point God in His mercy was kinder to me in this that what Origen did through imprudence, thereby incurring grievous censure, that He accomplished in me through no fault of my own. He thereby prepared me and made me free for a like work, and with less suffering for they laid hands on me quickly and suddenly when I was asleep and so felt little pain.

But the less I endured then, as it happened, from my mutilation, the longer am I now afflicted by their detraction and am tortured more by the loss of my reputation than I was from the mutilation of my body, for as it is written:[18] *Better is a good name than great riches.* And St. Augustine reminds us in a sermon[19] *on the Life and Morals of Clerics:*

> "The man who, relying on his own conscience, neglects his reputation is cruel. And just above he says: *We take forethought,* as the apostle says, *for what is honorable, not only before God, but also in the sight of men.* For ourselves our conscience suffices, for your sake our reputation should not be sullied but should exercise an influence among you... There are two things, conscience and reputation; conscience for yourself, reputation for your neighbor."

If they had lived in the time of Christ Himself and His members whether prophets, apostles or other holy fathers,

---

17 Cf. Eusebius, *Eccles. Hist.* VI, 8.
18 *Proverbs* XXII, 1.
19 Sermon 355; PL 39, 1569A.

what a charge my enemies would have brought against them when they saw them, though bodily intact, engaging with women in such close association! St. Augustine in his book[20] *On the Work of Monks* points out that women were such inseparable companions of the Lord Jesus Christ and the apostles that they accompanied them as they went forth to preach:

> "It was for this purpose that faithful women who had earthly goods went along with them and from their own means ministered to them that they might not be deprived of the necessities of life... If any one doubts that women of holy life went around with them wherever they preached the Gospel... let him listen to the Gospel and learn that they did this after the example of the Lord Himself... For it is written in the Gospel: *Then he was journeying through towns and villages ... proclaiming the good news of the kingdom of God, and with him were the twelve and certain women who had been cured of evil spirits and infirmities: Mary, who is called the Magdalene ... and Joanna, the wife of Chuza, Herod's steward and Susanna, and many others who used to provide for them out of their means.*"

And Leo the ninth in his treatise[21] *Against the Epistle of Parmenianus of the monastery of Studius* says :

---

20 PL 40, 552-3.

21 There is no such work of Leo IX extant. St. Augustine wrote a treatise against Parmenianus in three books entitled *Contra Epistolam Parmeniani* (PL 43, 33 ff.). I do not know how the name of Parmenianus crept into this text. The following extract is taken from the response of Cardinal Humbertus to a pamphlet written by Niceta, a monk from the monastery of Studius in Constantinople, against the Latins, entitled in the Latin translation (PG 120, 1011 ff.; PL 143, 973 ff.) *Libellus contra Latinos*. This passage is found in the *responsio* of Humbertus (PG 120, 1035D, 1036A and PL 143, 997D, 998A). It is also given in Gratian, *Decretum magistri Gratiani* (Leipsic, 1879), Dist. XXXI, c. XI and attributed to Leo IX with a note that Humbert was legate of Leo IX.

The monastery was founded by Studius (Studios) about 463. He was a Roman patrician and consul in 454. The monk Michael tells of the

"We profess outrightly that it is not lawful for a bishop, priest, deacon or subdeacon[22] to give up the care of his wife for the sake of religion so as not to provide for her food and clothing but he shall not know her carnally. So also we read the Holy Apostles acted as St. Paul says: *Have*[22a] *we not a right to take about with us a woman, a sister,... and the brethren of the Lord, and Cephas?* See, you fool, he does not say: Have we not a right 'to embrace' but 'to take around' a sister, a woman that their wives might be supported from the income of their preaching, not that there might be carnal intercourse between them."

Surely the Pharisee who said[23] to himself of the Lord: *This man, were he a prophet, would know who and what manner of woman this is who is touching him for she is a sinner*, could have imagined much more easily, so far as human judgments go, wrongdoing on the part of the Lord than they of me. Likewise with greater reason they could have harbored suspicion, if they had seen Christ's mother entrusted[24] to a young man or the prophets partaking as guests of the hospitality of widows.[25] What would those detractors of me have said if they had seen Malchus, the captive monk of whom St. Jerome writes,[26] living in the same dwelling with his wife? How much the more would they have made a crime of this which the

foundation by him of this monastery in his *Life of St. Theodore,* chapter 29; PG 99, 145AB. Cf. *Analecta Boll.* LII (1934), 64-65; *Lexicon für Theol. und Kirche* IX, 866-7.

[22] *Subdeacon* is in the manuscripts of the '*Historia Calamitatum*' and is also in the texts of the response of Humbertus in Migne but was left out of the text in the *Decree of Gratian* referred to above.

[22a] *I Cor.* IX, 5.

[23] *Luke* VII, 39.

[24] Cf. *John* XIX, 27.

[25] Cf. *III Kings* XVII, 10.

[26] Cf. *Vita Malchi;* PL 23, 56A.

illustrious doctor, upon seeing it, heartily commended saying:

> "In that region there was an old man by the name of Malchus... a native of that same place. There was an aged woman in his cottage... Both of them were so zealous in their religion and so wore down the threshold of the church that you would take them for Zachary and Elizabeth of the Gospel except that there was no John with them."

Why, tell me, do they refrain from speaking ill of the holy fathers of whom we frequently read or even see founding monasteries also for women and ministering to them after the example of the seven deacons[27] whom the apostles appointed in their place to look after the tables and the care of the women? The weaker sex needs the help of the stronger so that the Apostle always puts man over woman as the head. To signify the inferior position of woman he commands[28] her always to keep her head covered. And so I am somewhat surprised at the customs regarding monasteries now well-established whereby abbesses are placed over women just as abbots over men, and both men and women make their profession according to the same rule, though it is true that it contains many prescriptions which women, whether abbesses or nuns, can in no way carry out. Furthermore, in many places against the natural order, abbesses and nuns[29] are

---

[27] Cf. *Acts* VI.

[28] *I Cor.* XI, 4, 5.

[29] The system of double monasteries was two-fold. First, when a convent of women was subject to the abbot of a nearby monastery; we find these as far back as St. Basil's time in the East. The other, when a monastery of men was subject to the abbess of a nearby convent as at Whitby. This system was in vogue to some extent in France and Spain also. Cf. Dom U. Berlière, 'Les Monastères doubles au XII* et XIII* siècle, *Bulletin de l'Acad. royale de Belgique* XVIII, fasc. 3 (1923), 5-10; S. Hilpisch, *Die Doppelklöster, Entstehung und Organization* (Münster-in-Westph., 1928).

found ruling over clergy who in turn rule over the people; and they can the more easily lead men on to their evil desires, the greater the power they hold over them and the more rigidly they reduce them to subjection. As the Satirist[30] thoughtfully says: nothing is more intolerable than a woman who is rich.

Often considering my duty in their regard, I made up my mind to provide for the sisters as far as I could and to take care of them. And that they might revere me the more, I decided to be with them personally and to watch over them, thereby the better to meet their needs. While the persecution of my sons in religion was now becoming more frequent and intense than that of my brethen had formerly been, I kept repairing to my nuns as a haven of peace from this stormy tempest and gained some respite. I had accomplished nothing among my monks and felt I might do at least some good among them. And this would be as beneficial to me as it was necessary to them in their need.

But now Satan began to prevent me from getting a place where I could enjoy peace or even keep alive, but as a vagabond and refugee I was tossed about like the accursed Cain[31] since, as I mentioned above, I was incessantly buffeted by *conflicts without and anxieties within,* or rather by both alike from without and from within. The persecution of my sons against me became far more dangerous and constant than that of my open enemies. For they were always with me and without interruption I had to evade their plots. If I left the cloister, I saw

---

[30] Juvenal, *Satires* VI, 459.
[31] *Genesis* IV, 14.

that it would be at the risk of incurring bodily harm at
the hands of my enemies. While, if I remained within I
had to endure incessantly on the part of my sons, that is
my monks committed to me as their abbot, that is their
father, schemes as violent as they were treacherous. How
often they tried to poison me as happened in the case of
St. Benedict.[32] The same reason which led so great a
Father to leave his perverse sons openly encouraged me
after his example to do the same. For by exposing myself
to sure danger, I would prove myself to be rashly tempt-
ing God, not loving Him, and even become my own
destroyer.

While I guarded as best I could in food and drink
against their daily plots, they tried to do away with me
in the very sacrifice of the altar by putting poison in my
chalice.[33] One day I went to Nantes to visit the count
who was sick. I was staying with one my brothers and they
thought that there I would be less on my guard against
such a plot. So, working through a servant who was in
my retinue, they tried to poison me. But through God's
providence I did not touch the food which they had
prepared for me. A monk, however, whom I had brought
with me, without knowing it was poisoned, ate of it and
died right there and the servant who had been guilty of
such daring, from a sense of guilt and the bare-faced
fact, fled in terror.

From then on when their wickedness was so evident to
everybody, I openly began to forestall their plots as best

---

32 Cf. St. Gregory, *Dialogi* II, 3; PL 66, 136A; U. Moricca, *Gregorii
Magni Dialogi Libri IV* in *Fonti per la Storia d'Italia* (Istituto Storico
Italiano, Rome, 1924), p. 81.
33 Abelard certainly was a priest at this time.

I could and to withdraw myself from the enclosure of the abbey and to dwell with a few companions in small cells. If the monks figured I was going to go away somewhere, bribing some brigands to murder me, they posted them on the roads and byways. While I was struggling amidst these perils, the hand of the Lord strongly smote me. One day I happened to fall from my horse and broke a vertebra in my neck. This fracture afflicted and weakened me more grievously than the former injury.

I restrained the savage, rebellious spirit of some of the monks by excommunicating them. Others, of whom I was afraid, I compelled to give their word publicly under oath that they would get right out of the abbey and cause me no further trouble. They openly and shamelessly violated their sworn word until finally by authority of the Roman Pontiff through a special legate they were compelled, in the presence of the count and some bishops, to give an oath regarding this and many other matters. Even then they did not keep the peace. I got rid of those mentioned above, and, returning to the cloister of my abbey, I entrusted myself to the rest of the brethren of whom I was less suspicious. But they proved worse than the former. For they did not attack me with poison but drew a sword to my throat and I barely escaped from them under escort of a temporal prince.

And in this danger I am still involved and, as it were, see a sword dangling above my head so that I can scarcely be at ease at meals. I am like him of whom we read[34] who considered the power and acquired wealth of Dionysius the Tyrant happiness; but looking up, he saw a

[34] Cicero, *Tusc. Disp.* V, 21.

hidden sword hanging above the ruler by a thread and thereby learned what kind of happiness earthly power brings. That is my constant experience too, a poor monk made abbot, the more wretched as I became richer, that the ambition of those who wilfully seek the post may be checked by my example.

My beloved brother in Christ and close companion from our daily association, let this account of my misfortunes under which I have struggled, I might say, from the crib be an adequate summary to meet your discouragement and the wrong you have suffered so that, as I remarked in the beginning of my letter, you may count your affliction when compared to mine little or nothing. Regarding it as small, you will bear it with greater patience, always finding consolation in the words the Lord told[35] His members regarding the members of the devil: *If they have persecuted me, they will persecute you also. If*[36] *the world hates you, know that it has hated me before you. If you were of the world, the world would love what is its own. All who want,* says[37] the Apostle, *to live piously in Christ will suffer persecution.* And again,[38] *Or am I seeking to please men. If I were still trying to please men, I should not be a servant of Christ.* And the Psalmist:[39] They have been confounded who please men because God hath despised them.

Blessed Jerome, whose heir in calumny and detraction I see I am, paid special attention to these words when he

---

35 *John* XV, 20.
36 *John* XV, 18, 19.
37 *II Timothy* III, 12.
38 *Gal.* I, 10.
39 Cf. LII, 6.

wrote to Nepotianus:[40] *"If"*, says the Apostle, *"I were still trying to please men, I should not be a servant of Christ.* He ceases to please men and has become the servant of Christ". Likewise, when writing to Asella about false friends:[41] "I thank my God that I am counted worthy of the hatred of the world". And to Heliodorus the monk :[42]

> "My brother, you are mistaken, you are mistaken, if you suppose that there is ever a time when the Christian does not suffer persecution... Our adversary as a roaring lion, goes about seeking someone to devour, and do you think of peace? *He sitteth in ambush with the rich."*

And so fortified by this evidence and these examples, let us endure our crosses with greater resignation as they are the more unjust. Let us not hesitate, if not to gain merit, at any rate to make some progress in the purification of our soul. And since everything occurs by divine ordinance, let every faithful soul under every affliction find consolation in the thought that God in His great goodness never permits anything to occur outside His plan and that no matter what wrongdoing is done, He makes it work to the best issue. Wherefore in all things we are right in saying to Him: *Thy will be done.* What great consolation those who love God have on the authority of the Apostle who says:[43] *We know that for those who love God all things work together unto good.* The wisest of men carefully noted that when he said in the book of Proverbs:[44] *Whatsoever shall befall the just man, it shall not*

---

[40] *Epist.* LII, 13; PL 22, 537; CSEL 54, I, 1, p. 436.
[41] *Epist.* XLV, 6; PL 22, 482; CSEL 51, I, 1, p. 327.
[42] *Epist.* XIV, 4; PL 22, 349; CSEL 54, I, 1, p. 49.
[43] *Romans* VIII, 28.
[44] XII, 21.

make him sad. From this he shows that they clearly depart from righteousness who are wroth at some hardship which they have to bear, knowing full well that it comes upon them by divine dispensation. These follow their own will, not that of God, and through their secret desires they range themselves against the import of the words: *Thy will be done,* putting their own before the will of God. Farewell.